Alpha Jet

Alpha Jet

The Dassault/Dornier Alpha Jet is an aircraft that was designed for two purposes: to train future fighter pilots and as a small close support aircraft. In the latter role, the Alpha Jet A, it was mostly active in Germany, while as a trainer, it proved to be a successful aircraft in France, Belgium and other countries. The twin-engined trainer is an elegant aircraft, but make no mistake: it is highly agile and manoeuvrable and can take quite a lot of Gs. In the training role, it has a career of over 4 decades in Europe and while it is been taken out of service in some countries, it is about to start a second career in civil colours, as companies like Top Aces have been buying many of them to be used in the adversary role.

Today, many pilots flying the F-16 Fighting Falcon, Dassault Rafale and even some future F-35 pilots, had their first experience in a fast jet with the Alpha Jet. In Belgium for example, it was a big step to go from the SIAI Marchetti SF.260 to the Alpha Jet, but a necessary one on the way to become a fighter pilot. Able to fly at 1,000 km/h, the thrill of flying in the small trainer is one to never forget.

This book is a tribute to the Alpha Jet, an aircraft on which hardly any good book has been made in such detail. We are proud to show you every side of it and you will see that it holds some pretty cool features. For this book, Robert Pied took the lead and made a huge amount of photos. We have to thank Bart Rosselle, the official air-to-air photographer of the Belgian Air Force for allowing us to use some of his fantastic photos. All photographers listed below are not only very talented, but also true aviation enthusiasts. As we know you must be too. Time to get in the seat and get the engines running!

Photo: Bart Rosselle

Special thanks to these gentlemen, all good-looking: Robert Pied, Marco Casaleiro, Bart Rosselle, Guillaume Friart, Jens Schymura, Philip Stevens, Kris Christaens, Jorge Ruivo, Teerawut Wongdee, Volkhard Waltermann, Brendon Attard and Gunter Geens

Above: A Portuguese Air Force Alpha Jet A is banking to the left - all Portuguese aircraft are former Luftwaffe jets and are used in the training role, in which they replaced the T-38 Talon. The A version can be easily recognised by the pointed nose with the small pitot tube, compared to the trainer version, or Alpha Jet E, which has a more rounded nose, making the aircraft look a little like a dolphin. Well, that's what I feel...

Left: An Alpha Jet of the Armée de l'Air is taxiing back after a training sortie at Cazaux, near Bordeaux on the Atlantic coast.

Photo: Marco Casaleiro

Photo: Robert Pied

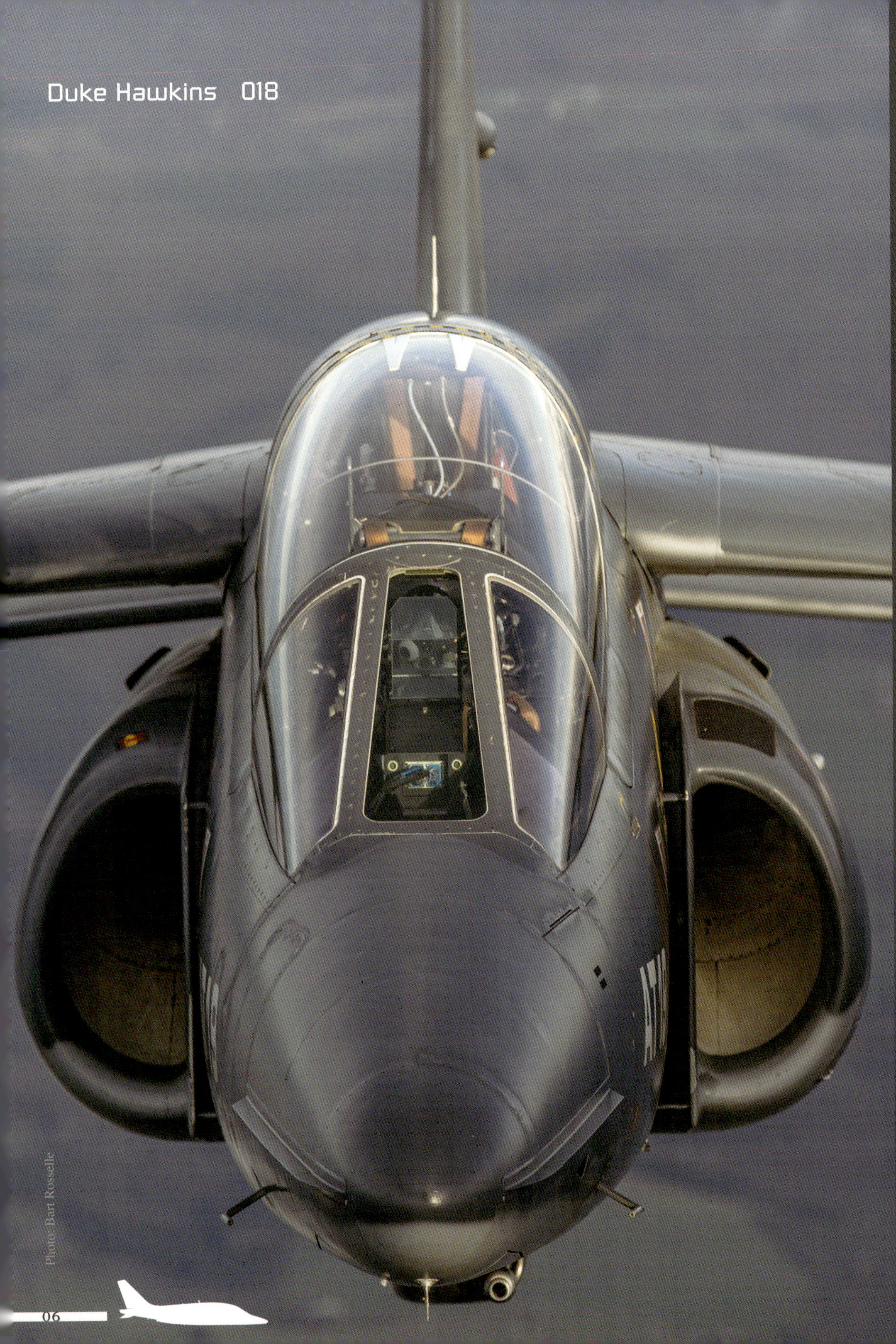

Photo: Bart Rosselle

Photo: Bart Rosselle

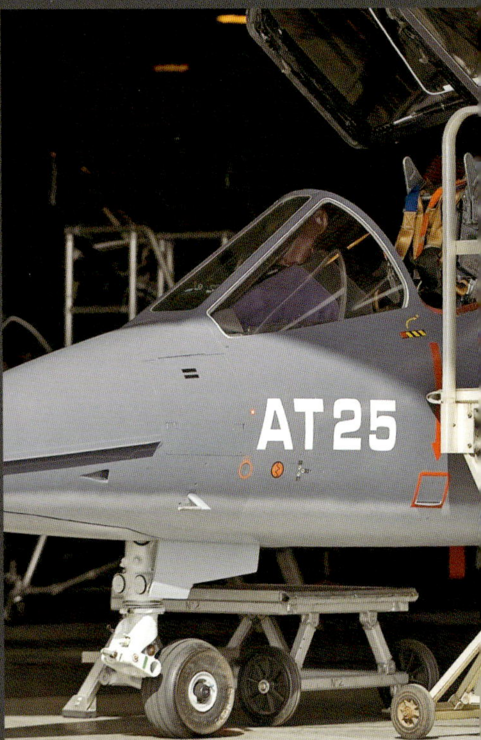

Usually, we spend some time explaining the different types of the aircraft we present, but in this case, we were able to do it in the introduction, so let's jump right into the details of the aircraft - as usual, we begin with the forward fuselage.

The Alpha Jet is a small aircraft, measuring just under 12 meter long with a wing span of 9,11 meter. Everything in the design is made to train the pilot: a large cockpit with a lot of glass to give a good all-around vision, an instructor that sits higher, so he can have a view forward, and good aerodynamics. The photo to the left shows a head-on view of the Alpha Jet, with its large air intakes and high positioned wings.

Photo: Bart Rosselle

: Robert Pied

Training thousands of pilots

Although flying the Alpha Jet is still a long way from flying a combat jet, the aircraft enables the student-pilot to gain some very important techniques. In the aircraft's long career, thousands of pilots got to experience the thrills of flying their first solo in a jet. This training involved basic excercises, but also instrument flying, combat training, and more.

Left: The nose of the Alpha Jet E with the horizontal metal vanes running along them. These strips allow the aircraft to execute spins, an essential part of the training. Notice the pitot-tube positionned above the nose landing gear door.

Above: This photo shows the windscreen with the two reinforcement bars. Early Alpha Jet didn't have a HUD - Head-Up Display - but during a midlife update, the Belgian and later French aircraft did get the system. Look how paint has been chipped off the braces and the screws on them. The Belgian Air Force took delivery of the first Alpha Jet in December of 1978; exactly 40 years later, the type was withdrawn from service without a successor appointed to take over the task of training future fighter pilots. Today, Belgian student-pilots are trained in the USA on T-38 and Texan IIs, flying out of Sheppard AFB in Texas.

And here's one of those fantastic photos by Bart Rosselle - look at all the detail captured in this shot: the nose with the pitot tube, the LOX compartment above it and the steps to get into either of the cockpits. This Alpha Jet is equipped with the DEFA gun pod fixed underneath the fuselage. Notice how the ejection seat in the front has larger canopy breakers on top than the one in the back.

13
DANGER
DANGER
DANGER
rescue
TO FREE PILOT
WARNING

Photo: Marco Casaleiro

Photo: Duke Archives

Photo: Robert Pied

Above: A Portuguese Alpha Jet equipped with a pair of droptanks and a gun pod, taxis towards the runway on a rainy morning.

Left: Belgian Air Force Lt. Col. Marc Scheers has put his helmet on the canopy release handle after a training flight with AT-24, the Alpha Jet nicknamed "Dark Bat", to fill in some paperwork. The symbol and numbers on his helmet remind of his previous post, when he flew F-16s with 349 Squadron.

Below: This photo shows how low the airframe of the Alpha Jet really is. There is no need for a ladder to get into the cockpit. The student-pilot has only to take one step - notice the red arrow - to get into his seat. The canopy is opened by using the black-and yellow striped handle. The instructor in the back takes three steps, two of which are located on the side of the air intake, the third is on top of it. The updated version of the Alpha Jet provides a HUD Repeater for the instructor, making forward view even better.

Photo: Kris Christiaens

Right: An additional step for the front cockpit slides out of the lower fuselage.

Far right: Both canopies are released by means of this type of handle on the port side of the fuselage. First you push the red button, which makes the handle pop out; then you pull and turn it upwards 90 degrees.

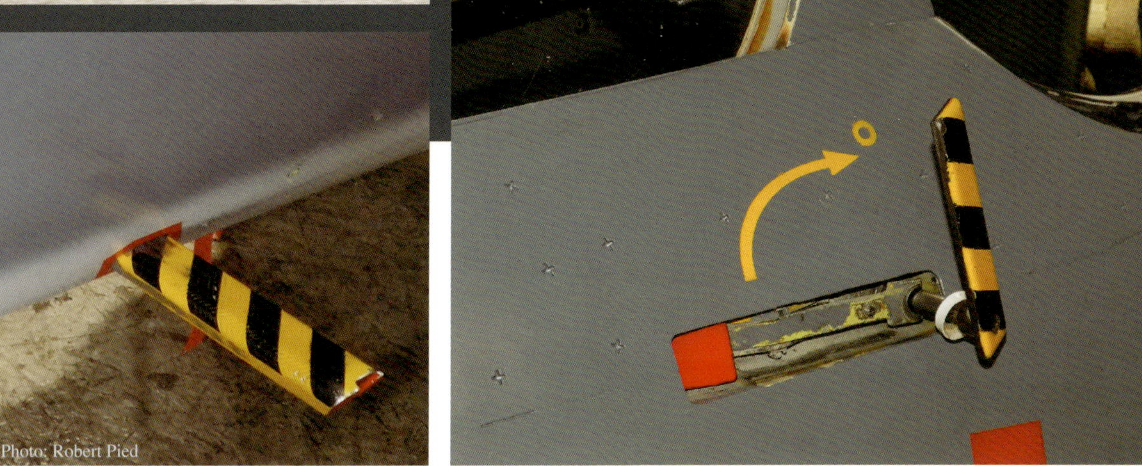

Photo: Robert Pied

Photo: Robert Pied

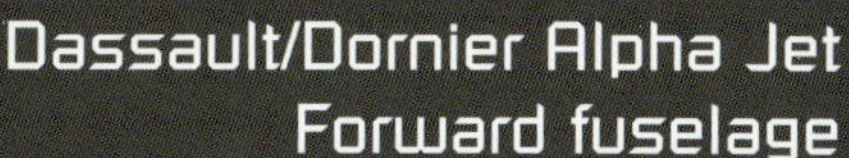

Left: This photo shows the fuselage framing on the port side of the forward cockpit. Notice where the hooks fit that close and secure the canopy. Above: The forward canopy is opened by pushing the red button, pulling the yellow-and-black lever and turning it upwards.

Photo: Duke Archives

In 2004, the Belgian Air Force and the French Armée de l'Air started AJets, a program in which they would train future fighter pilots together. Both the Belgian and French Alpha Jets were transfered to Cazeaux AB, near Bordeaux in France. The photo to the right shows a French Alpha Jet preparing for take-off from RAF Lakenheath in 2008. The French aircraft was flown by a Belgian crew at RAF Lakenheath as part of flight training for the crew. Notice the early style ejector seats and the roundels on the air intake/landing gear door.

Photo: Sr Airman Brian J. Ellis · USAF

Right: In case of an emergency on the ground, crew can liberate the pilots by breaking the glass window and pulling the handle inside. This will active the charges on the outer parts of the canopy - the Peripheral Charges - This emergency system is located on either side of the fuselage. Pilots can activate it also from inside the aircraft.

Photo: Duke Archives

Photo: Duke Archives

Photo: Robert Pied

Photo: Guillaume Friart

Far left: Have a closer look at this photo to notice the explosive charges placed on the forward canopy. The charges are light grey lines, with the most visible the ones on top of the canopy, which are the overhead charges that are activated during ejection. Following the canopy framing are the Peripheral charges that are activated in case of an emergency on the ground.

Left: An air intake is located on the port side of the nose, immediately below the horizontal strake.

Export Success

The Alpha Jet proved to be an successful export product, mainly because of the combination of good handling, small size and afordable price. The biggest operators were France, Germany and Belgium, but many other countries purchased the type and some continue to fly it, decades after it was introduced. Both Morocco and Nigeria bought 24 aircraft, Egypt bought two batches totalling 52 aircraft. After Germany retired its 93 Alpha Jet As, 50 of them were bought by Portugal. Other countries include Thailand, Qatar, Togo, Ivory Coast aand the UK, where 12 former Luftwaffe aircraft operatd with QinetiQ until 2018. Left: This head-on photo, taken while lying on the ground in the maintenance hangar of Beauvechain AB in Belgium, shows the nose with the Tacan Aerial and the off-centre nose landing gear.

Photo: Bart Rosselle

Photo: Duke Archives

13

Photo: Jens Schymura

Above: A Portuguese Alpha Jet A is taxiing back after a flight and has its large speed brakes open. Contrary to the E-version - E stands for Ecole or School - of the aircraft, the A- version - Attack - is often equipped with underwing pylons, which can be loaded with additional fuel tanks, transport pods or weapons.

Right: The biggest difference in appearance between the A and the E is the nose of the aircraft. A-type aircraft have a pointy nose with a pitot-tube at the end of it. This photo shows the forward fuselage of an Alpha Jet A of the former Portuguese demo team Asas de Portugal, hence the special livery. Notice the black antenna on the side and the Angle of Attack antenna on top of the nose.

Photo: Jens Schymura

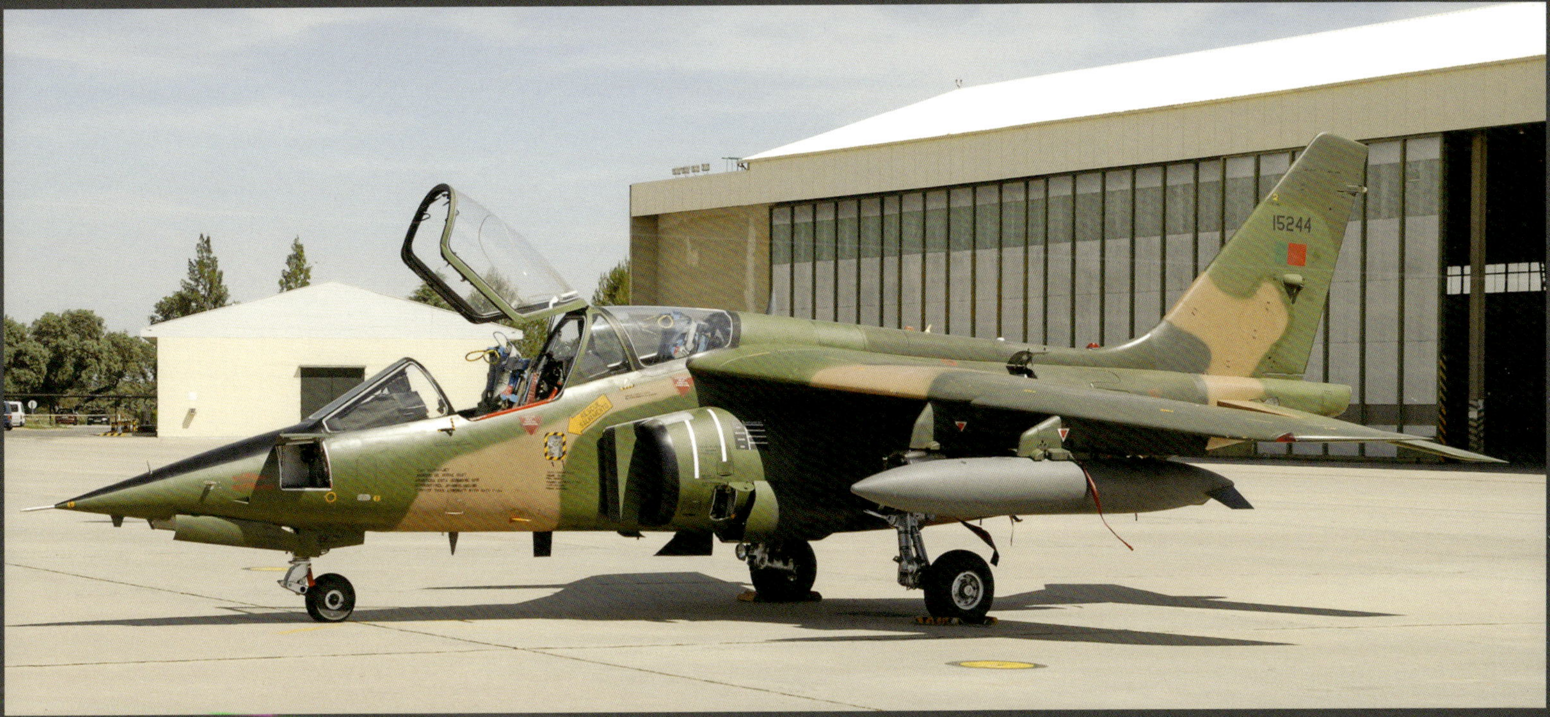

Photo: Jens Schymura

Above: A particularly clean Portuguese Alpha Jet is just about ready for another training mission. It has some of the inspection panels open and an open transport container on the port inner pylon. The open panel near the windscreen houses the LOX - Liquid Oxygen for the crew. See page 80 for a more close-up look of the panel and the interior of it. The forward parts of the air intakes and splitter plate are painted black, as is the area in front of the windscreen.

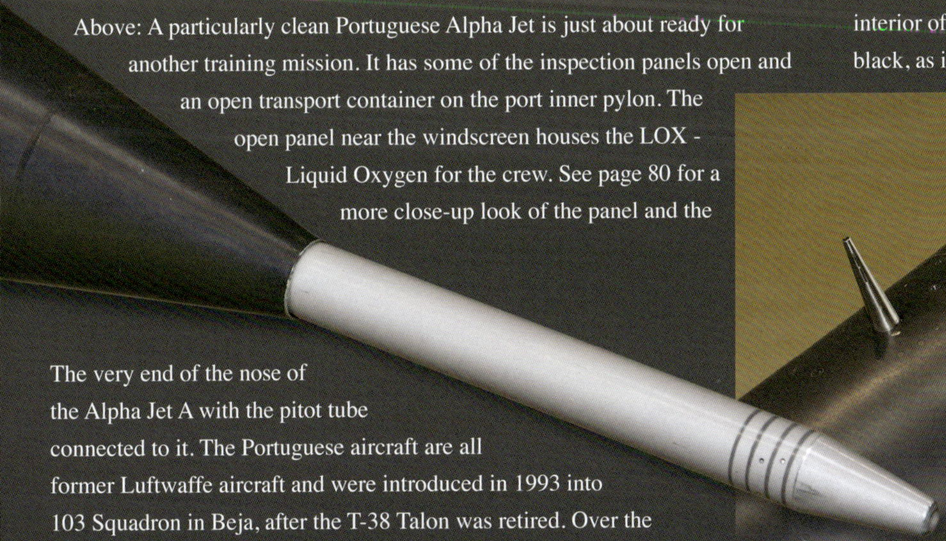

The very end of the nose of the Alpha Jet A with the pitot tube connected to it. The Portuguese aircraft are all former Luftwaffe aircraft and were introduced in 1993 into 103 Squadron in Beja, after the T-38 Talon was retired. Over the course of the years, some aircraft were withdrawn and by the end of 2017, just 6 remained in operational status. On January 13, 2018, the last of the type were retired. For 103 Squadron, this was the end of the line, after having flown legendary jets as the F-84G, T-33 Shooting Star and the T-38 Talon.

Photo: Jens Schymura

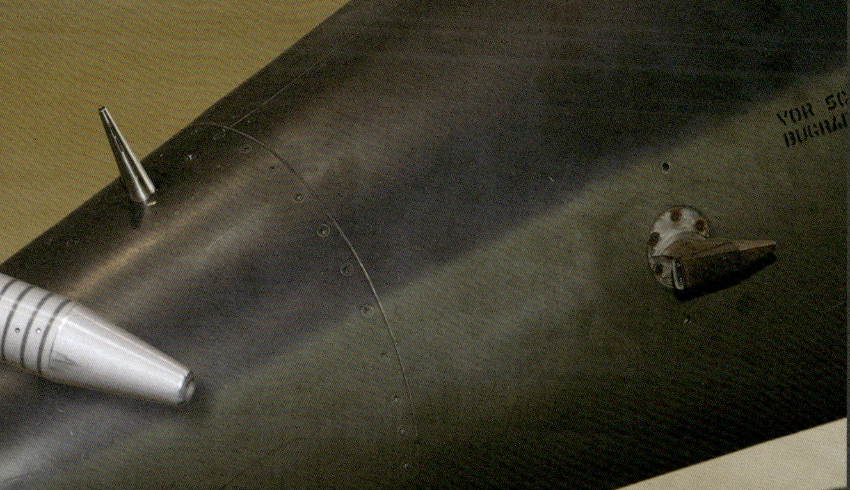

Above: A close-up of the nose with an instrument probe to the side and the AOA - Angle of Attack - probe on top of the fuselage. This photo is of a preserved Luftwaffe Alpha Jet A.

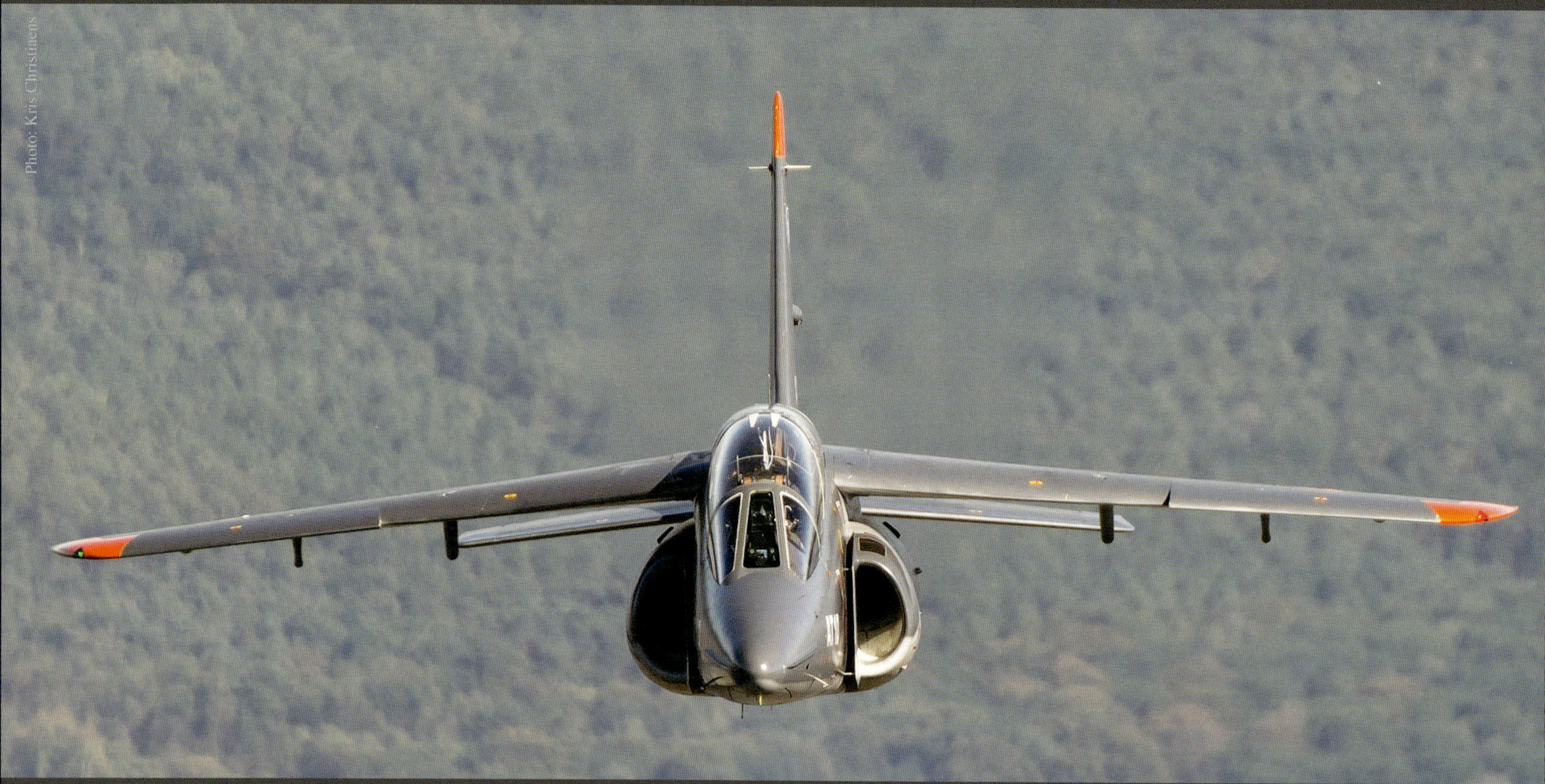

Photo: Kris Christiaens

Photo: Robert Pied

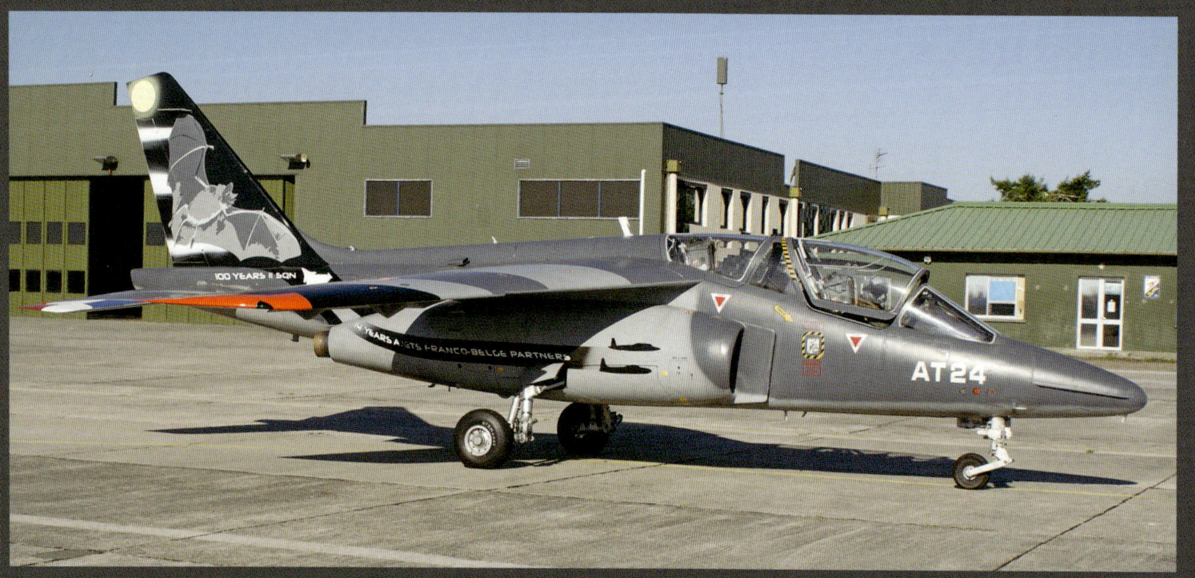

Above: This Belgian Air Force Alpha Jet is lining up with a C-130 for an air-to-air photo shoot. Look at the position and shape of the air intakes and shoulder-high wings. The aircraft is powered by a pair of SNECMA Turbomeca Larzac 04-C5 turbofan engines, giving it a maximum thrust of just under 3,000 lbs each.

Left: AT-24 seen in profile shows how small the air-intake and engine nacelle actually is. The engine itself is just 1,18 meter long and weighs only 295 kg.

Some photos showing the port and starboard air intake, with a splitter plate fixed to it. Notice the structure inside of the intake in the photo below. Both intakes are almost a mirror of each other, in that regard that the port one has crew access steps in it and the starboard one has a refuelling point in it.

Below left: Before starting the process of refuelling, the electrostatic connection point has to be secured. Refuelling has to be done at the right speed - no faster than 3.5 bars, which is 35 Cu. feet per minute.

Advanced training

The step from a single engine piston aircraft, such as the SIAI Marchetti SF.260 to the twin-engined Alpha Jet is huge for student pilots. With a top speed of 940 km/h and take off speed of 195 km/h, it can leave quite an impression on the young pilots. Once basic flying has been learned, future fighter pilots have to pass general flight, instrument flying, navigation, formation flying, night flying, tactical flying and between 30 and 50 hours in the flight simulator.

Above: On top of the port air intake, sand-paper like material is fixed, making sure that the instructor doesn't slip when he/she steps into the cockpit. The crew boards the jet always from the port side, where the steps are located in the forward fuselage and forward air intake.

Above, right: In between the air intake and the fuselage, a pair of strengthener struts can be found; one near the top, the other near the bottom. Right: This photo shows the entire depth of the starboard air intake - notice that the engine has been removed. Some 30 cm inside the intake the surface is painted white.

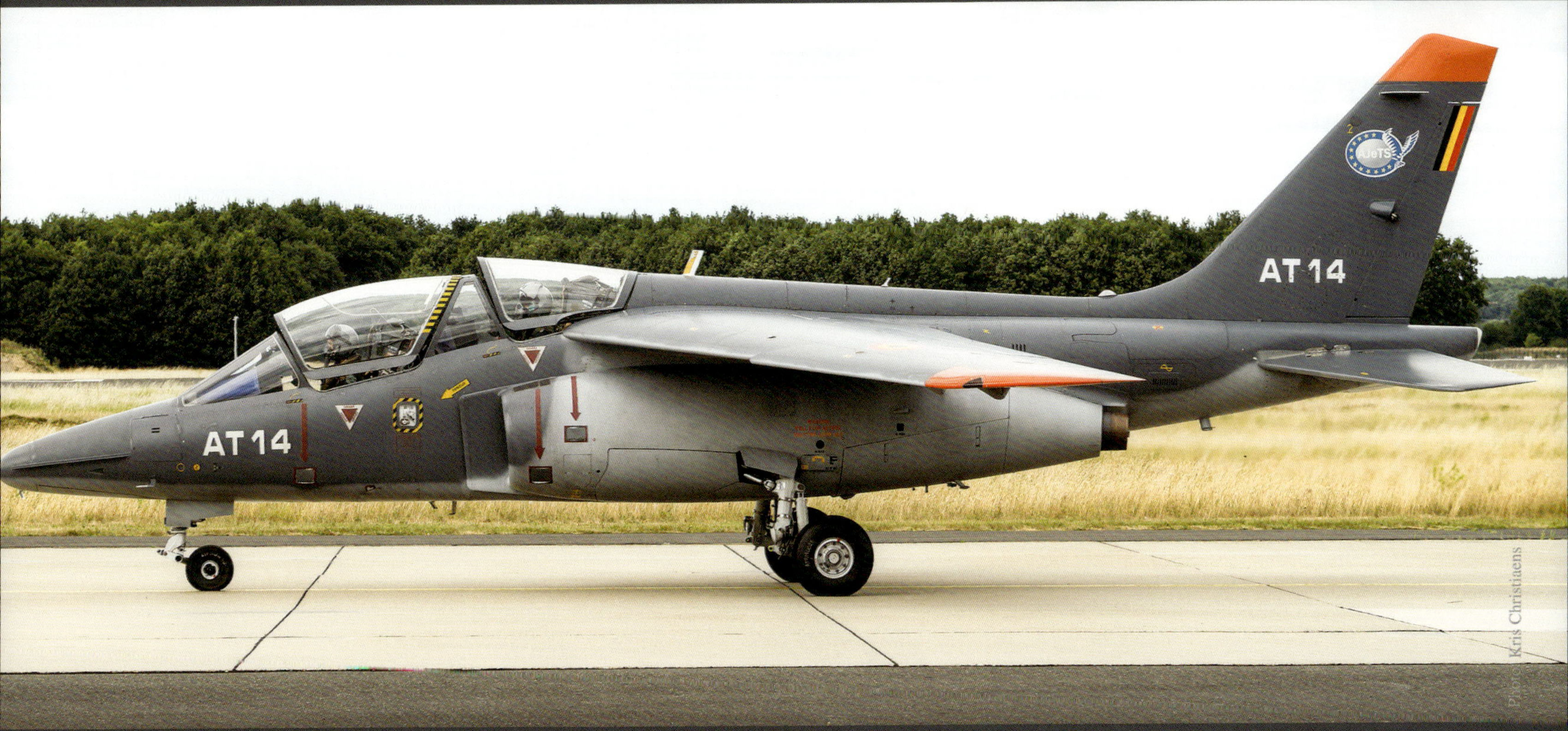

Photo: Kris Christiaens

Photo: Robert Pied

Photo: Duke Archives

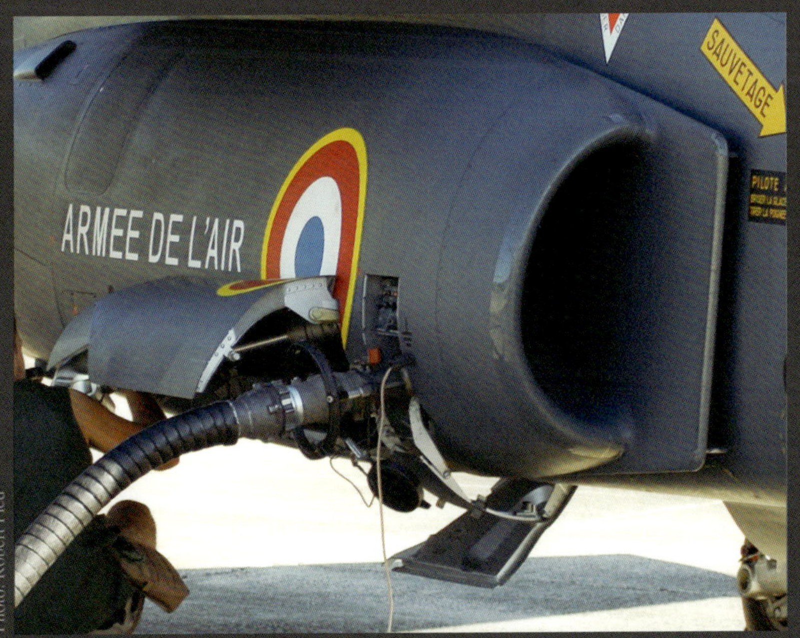

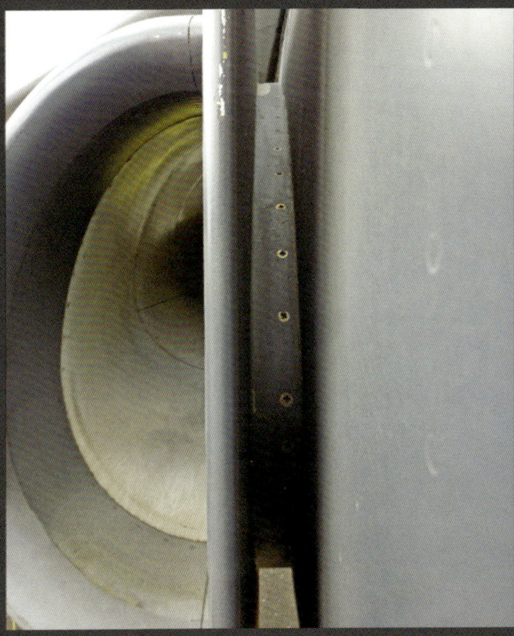

Above: Another profile photo, this time from the port side. Notice the dayglo fin and wing tips.
Far left: This French Alpha Jet is being refuelled. On top of the aircraft, near the trailing edge base of the port wing, a gravity refuelling point is located
Left: The area between the fuselage and the air intake.

Photo: Robert Pied

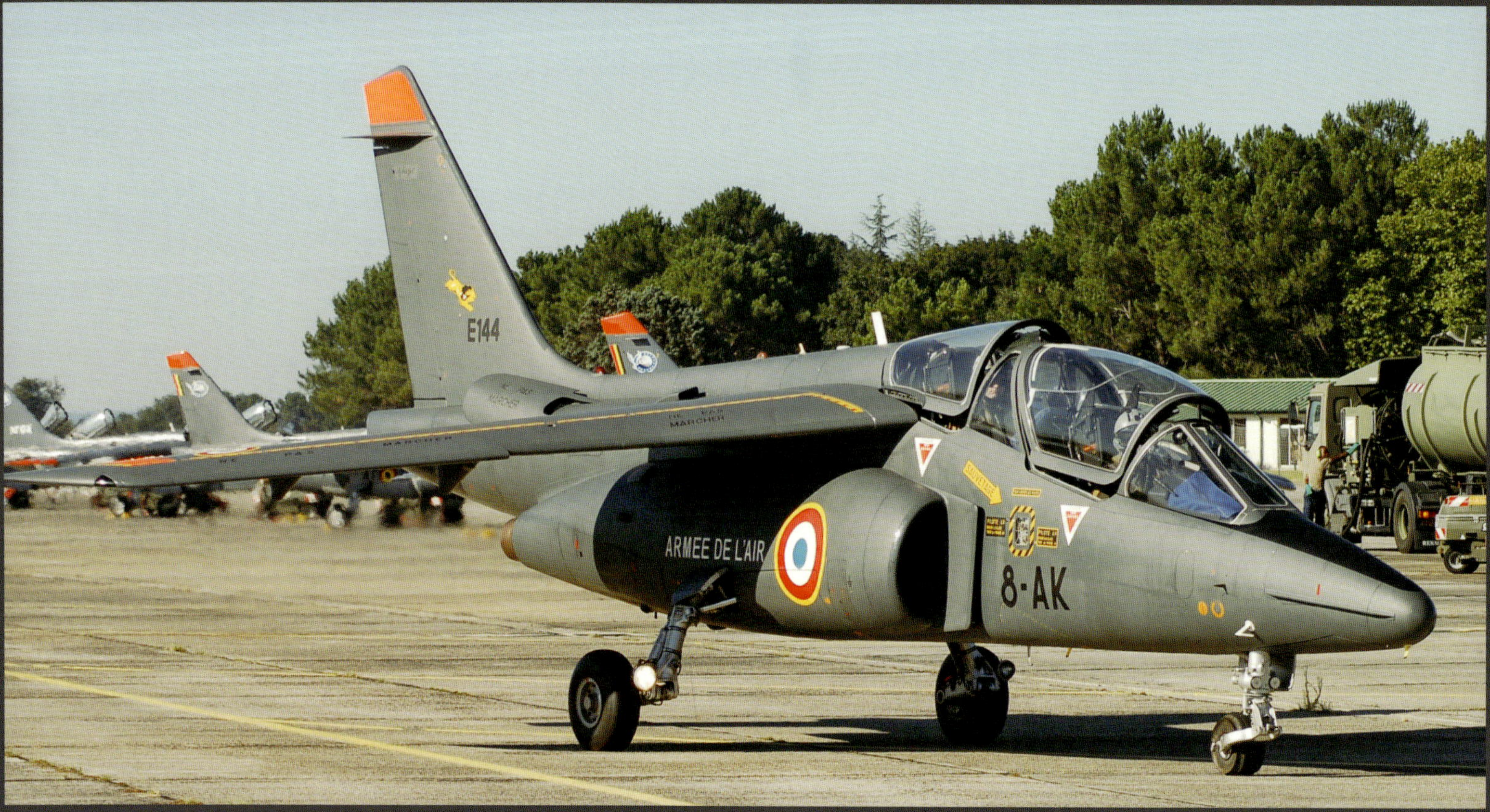

Above: Cazaux, France in the summer of 2018 and one of the AJets is coming back from a training exercise. Notice the partly deployed speed brakes and large canopies.

Right: This photo shows the backseat cockpit - we'll get to that part of the jet in detail further in this book - and how close it is to the center of the aircraft. Look how far the wing root goes next to it and how part of the canopy framing is shaped to go flush with it. This Belgian Alpha Jet is equipped with Martin-Baker Mk.10 ejection seats, of which the one in the back has much smaller canopy breakers than the one in the front cockpit.

Photo: Robert Pied

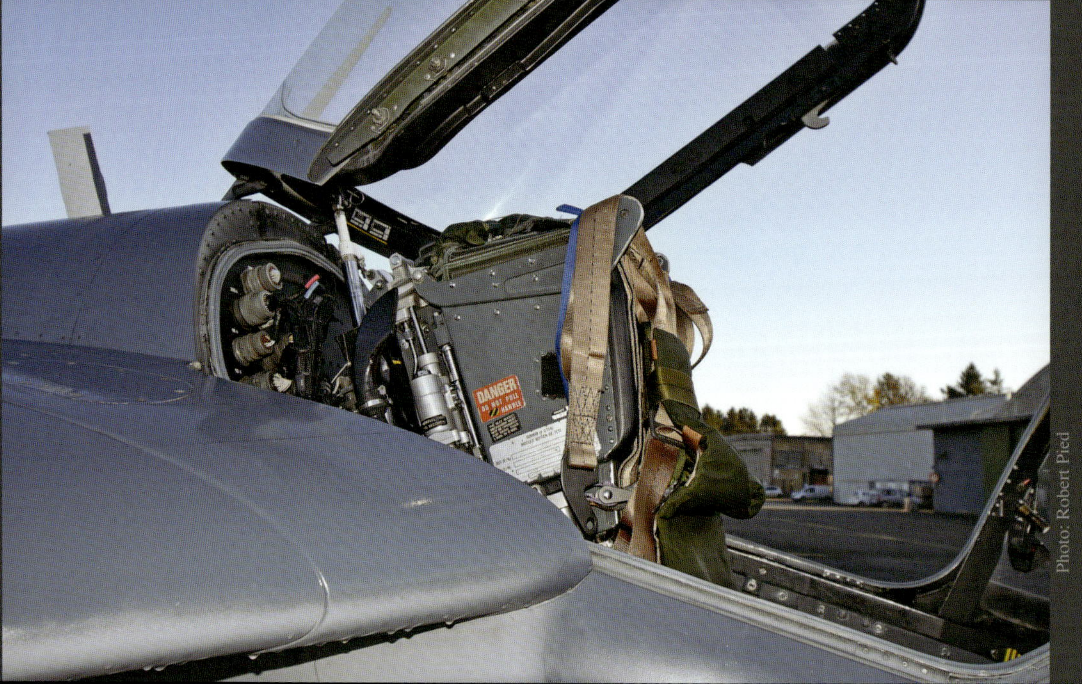

A French Alpha Jet, based at Cazaux, at the Atlantic coast near Bordeaux, is passing at high speed and low level through the Mach Loop in Wales. This awesome photo by Philip Stevens shows to good effect how compact the Alpha Jet actually is; the instructor in the back is almost sitting halfway through the fuselage. The two engines and large wings make the jet trainer very agile and responsive. Take your time to look closely at the photo - see the effects of the jet exhausts and the turbulence at the wing tips?

Photo: Philip Stevens

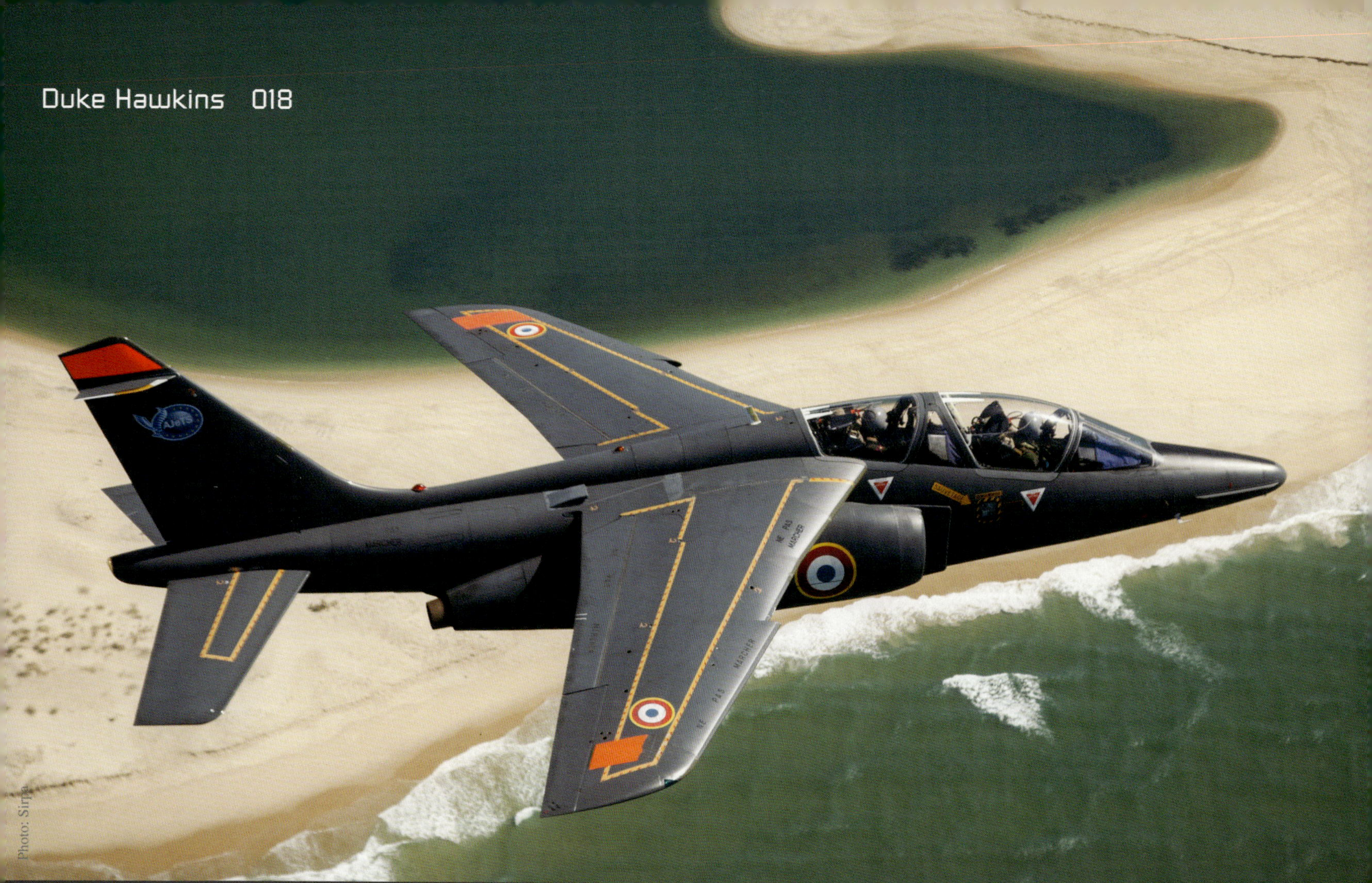

Photo: Sirpa

Photo: Nigerian Air Force

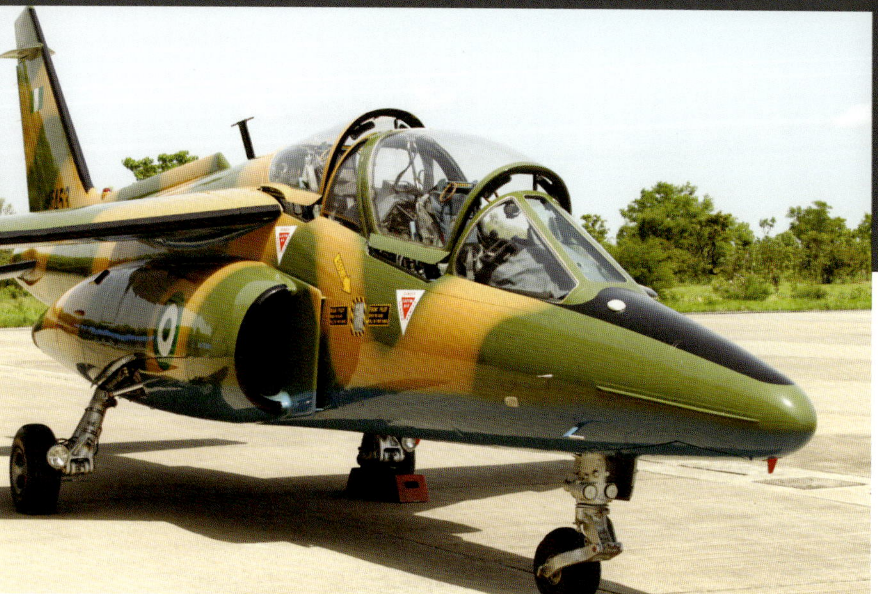

Above: A French Alpha Jet - look at the old type of ejection seats - is passing over the Atlantic coast near its home base of Cazaux. Notice the structure of the top fuselage and the wings; near the base of the starboard wing, an inlet for cooling air can be seen. Yellow and red lines indicated where the ground crew and mechanics are allowed to walk on top of the aircraft.

Left: Originally, Nigeria operated 24 Alpha Jets, which were used extensively in the 1990s, mostly in close air support missions. The Nigerian aircraft have a lengthened base of the vertical tail, running far forward on the spine of the jet. As of 2013, 13 of the Alpha Jets were brought back into service and upgraded, because of the urgent need for strike capability in the fight against jihadist terrorist organisation Boko Haram, which operates in the northern part of the country.

Above: This is what the cooling air inlet on top of the fuselage, near the base of the wings looks like when seen from the front. This is only to be found on the starboard side of the fuselage.

Above: AT-24 sits in the sun, waiting for one of the last training flights of it's career. It is the summer of 2018 and in a few months, the aircraft will be retired from active service before it will be shipped across the Atlantic to start a new life with Top Aces. On the air intake, silhouettes of it's predecessors are painted: the Fouga Magister and T-33 Shooting Star.

Right: A ground crew technician checks whether the air intake is clear and free of FOD. Notice the position of the main landing gear doors.

Photo: Robert Pied

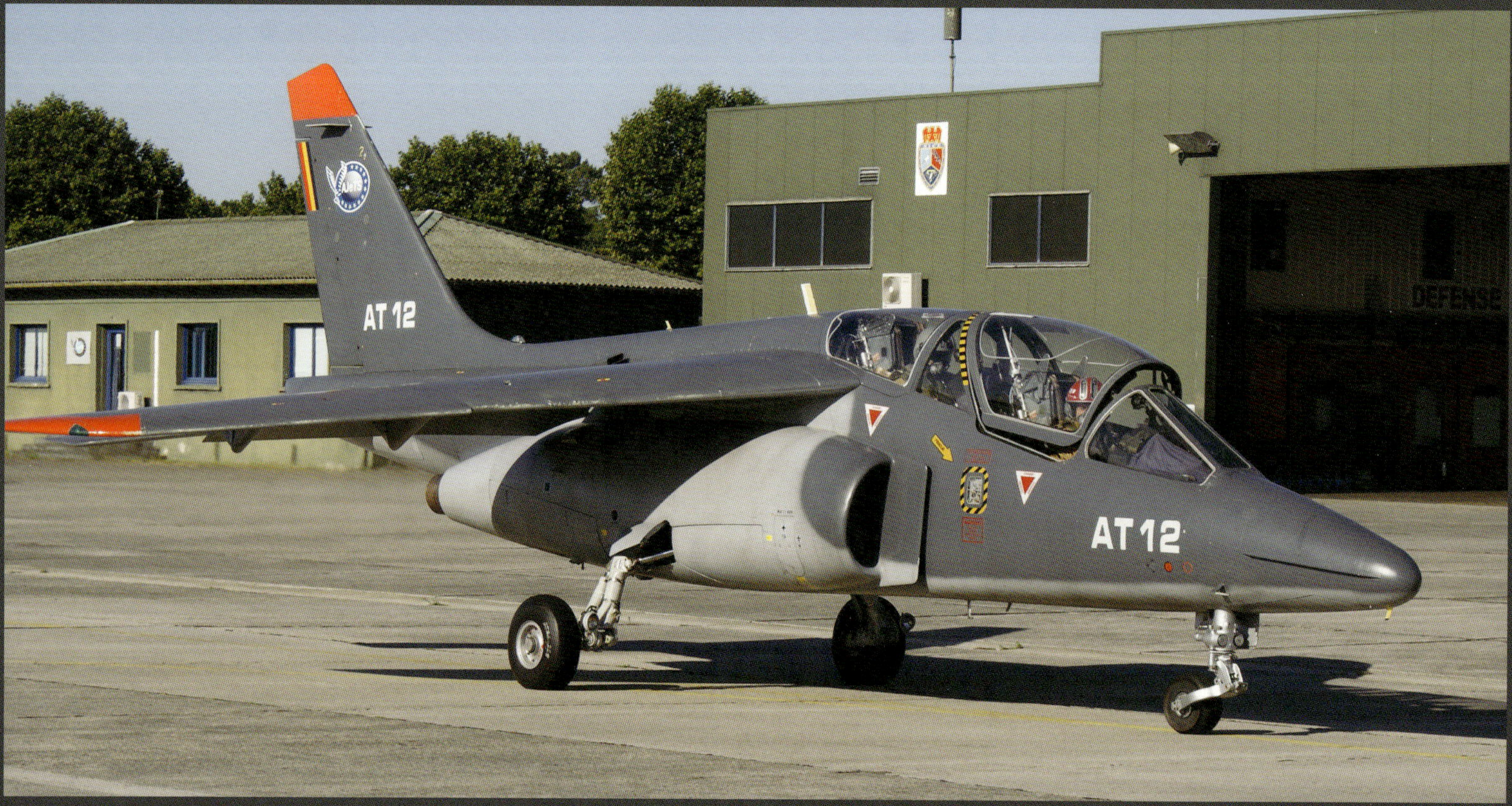

Above: On the spine of the Alpha Jet two antenna can be found: the larger one in the front is the UHF aerial and the smaller one further aft is the IFF antenna.
Left: A close-up of the IFF antenna on the spine of the aircraft.
Far left: A look at the spine and the wing-fuselage connection. Look how smooth the surface is.

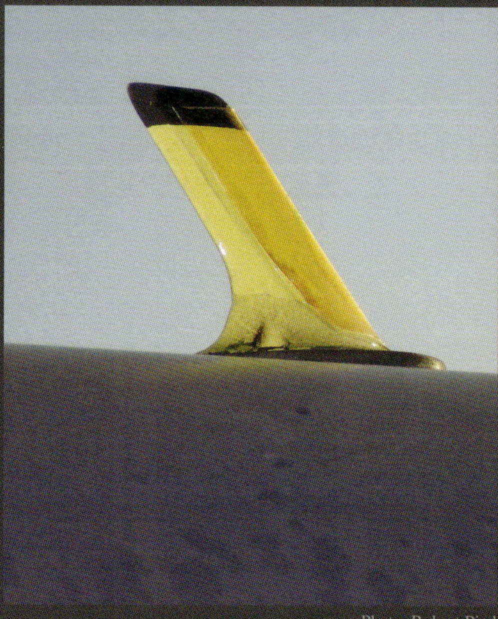

Photo: Robert Pied

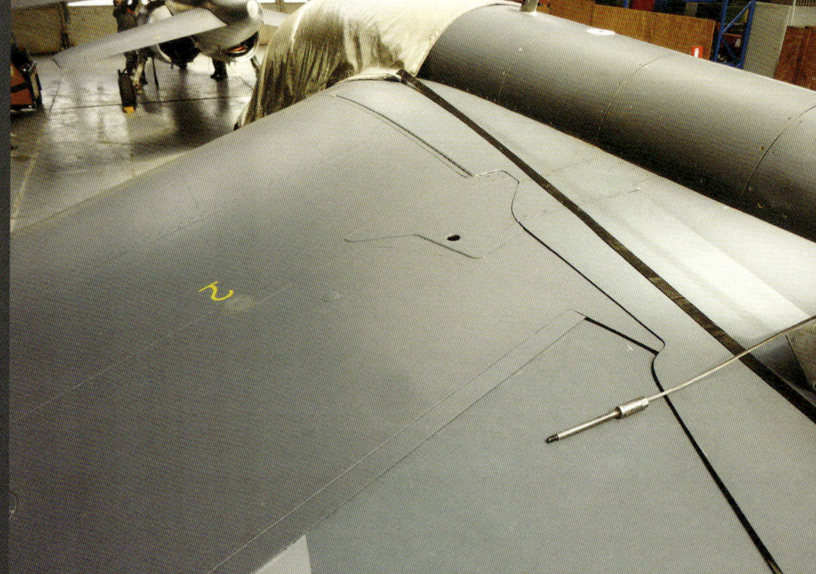

Photo: Duke Archiv

Above: This French AJets has a pair of external fuel tanks installed on the outboard wing pylons. Near the base of the vertical tail, a navigation light is situated, with another one in the middle of the spine. This differs from the Belgian aircraft, that only have one near the base.

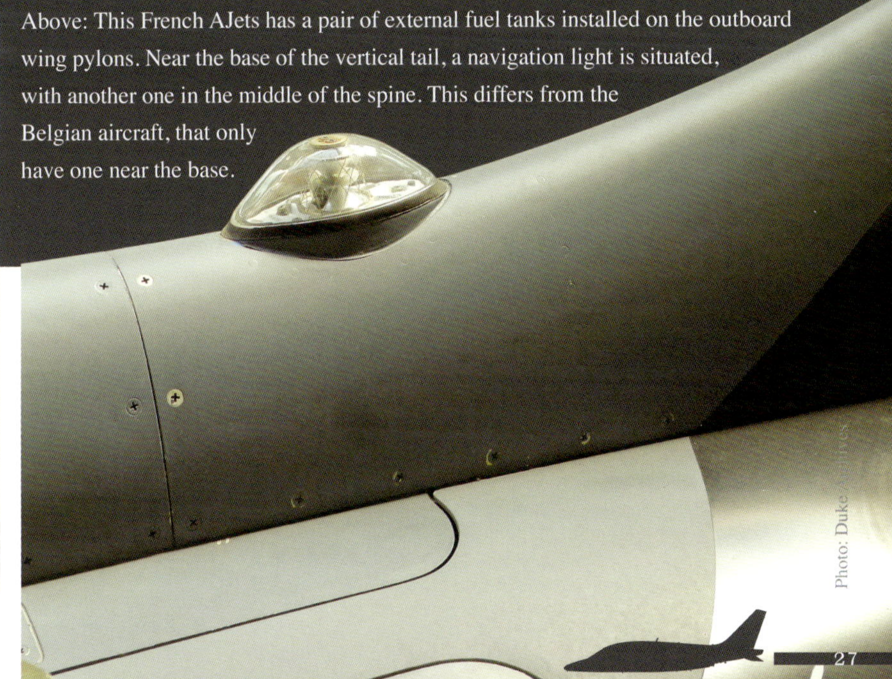

Photo: Philip Stevens

Photo: Robert Pied

Photo: Duke Stevens

27

Above: A pair of Belgian Alpha Jets break from behind the photo ship. Notice the gun pod mounted underneath the jet in the lead.

The Air Force of Cameroon purchased Alpha Jet MS2 aircraft early in the 1980s, which is an upgraded version of the Alpha Jet MS1. This version has more powerful engines and the capacity to use air-to-air missiles. Take a closer look at the aircraft in this photo; they have the initial ejection seats and a TMV630 laser rangefinder in the modified nose. Apart from Cameroon, only Egypt had this type of the Alpha Jet in service. I like the camouflage scheme of these a lot ...

Photo: Bart Rosselle

Photo: Cameroon Air Force

Above: An Alpha Jet of the Armée de l'Air passes at high speed through the Mach Loop in Wales, wearing a three-tone camouflage.

Right: Because of the agility and manoeuvrability, the Alpha Jet proved to be a popular aircraft for aerobatics. Both France and Belgium had several Display Teams flying the jet. Here a French Solo Display pilot is in his finals for landing.

Above: Not an everyday sight - this is an Alpha Jet of the Royal Thai Air Force, carrying a special decoration on the vertical tail to commemorate the centennial of the Air Force. The aircraft - all 25 of them - are former Luftwaffe Alpha Jets, hence the pointed nose and the early style ejection seats. I have to say that they look pretty cool in this three-tone grey wrap-around camouflage!

Right: This photo shows the port side of the fuselage and underside of the wing to good effect. Notice how the main landing gear doors are closed except for a small one over the gear struts.

Photo: Teerawut Wongdee

Photo: Duke Archives

Left: The aft fuselage and engine nacelle with the engines removed. Look how quick-release buttons open the large engine bay door to give access to the Larzac 04-C5 turbofan engine. This photo shows the location of the ground power and hydraulics hook-up, in front of the engine door - the photo below shows a close-up of it. To the left are the hydraulics hook-up, to the right the connections for the electrical supply.

Below left: The Exhaust Overflow and overpressure release for the fuel tanks.

Photo: Duke Archives

Photo: Robert Pied

Photo: Marco Casaleiro

Shoulder high Wings

The Alpha Jet has a wingspan of 9.11 meter and the wings of the aircraft are canted downwards. The wings don't have leading edge slats, but they each have a single large trailing edge flap. In spite of the lack of slats and the fixed air intake, the design of the wings, which was developed with the aid of CAD - Computer Aided Design - made sure that performance was optimal. Flaps, rudder and all other flight control surfaces are hydraulically operated, ensuring a responsive and agile aircraft, ideal for pilot training and close air support missions.

The flaps are activated by means of a pair of actuators with a distinctive triangular shape. The ailerons are operated by a single actuator with an aerodynamic cover. The photo above of a Portuguese Alpha Jet A of the Asas de Portugal, captures the actuators of both flaps and aileron. Look how the horizontal tails are canted down in a slightly higher angle than the wings.

Above: This photo shows how close the trailing edge flap comes to the fuselage when it is fully down. The inside of the flap of the Alpha Jet A is shaped to the curve of the engine bay.
Above right: The lowered port flap and the actuator mechanism on the inside of it.

Right: A French Alpha Jet E is taxiing by with the trailing edge flap lowered. Notice that the horizontal tail is all-moving.

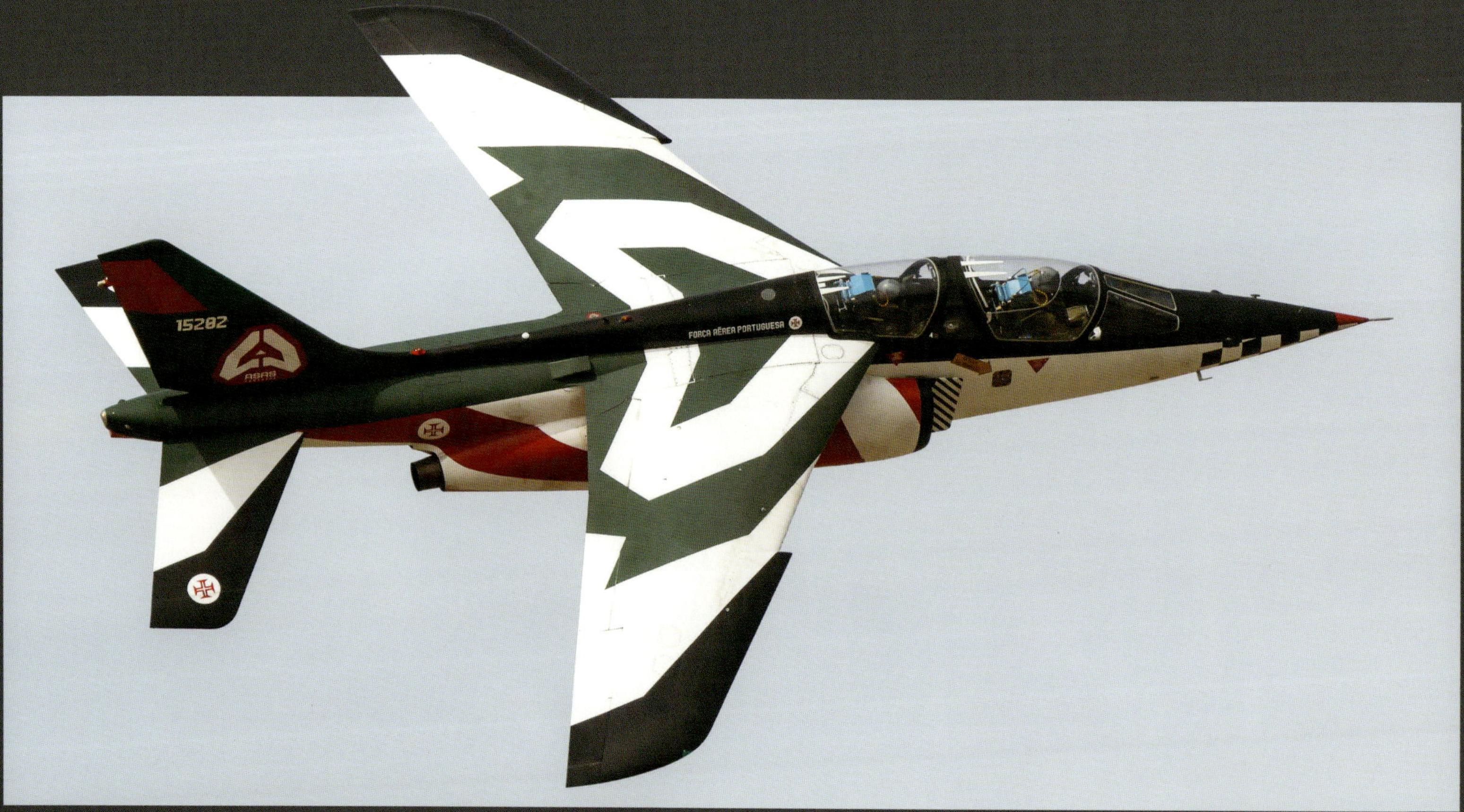

Photo: Marco Casaleiro

Above: This great shot by Marco Casaleiro shows the entire wing surface of a Portuguese Alpha Jet in the livery of the Asas de Portugal.

Below: Compare this photo to the one on page 33 - this shows the port wing base of the Alpha Jet E. Notice some of the open panels on the fuselage.

Photo: Duke Archives

Photo: Duke Archives

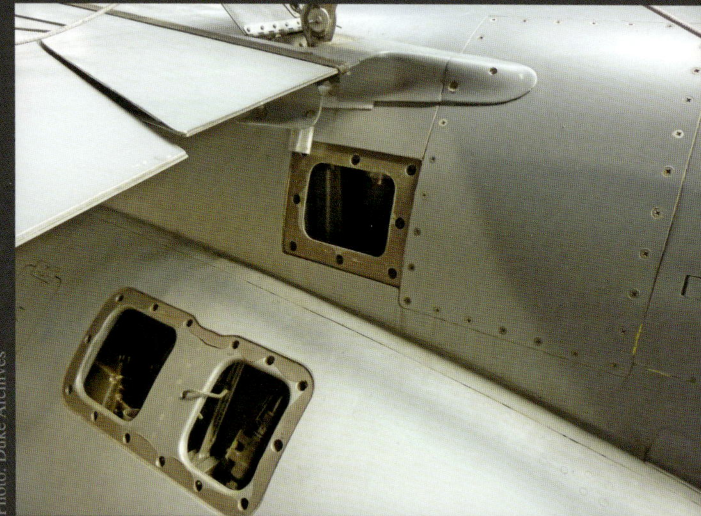

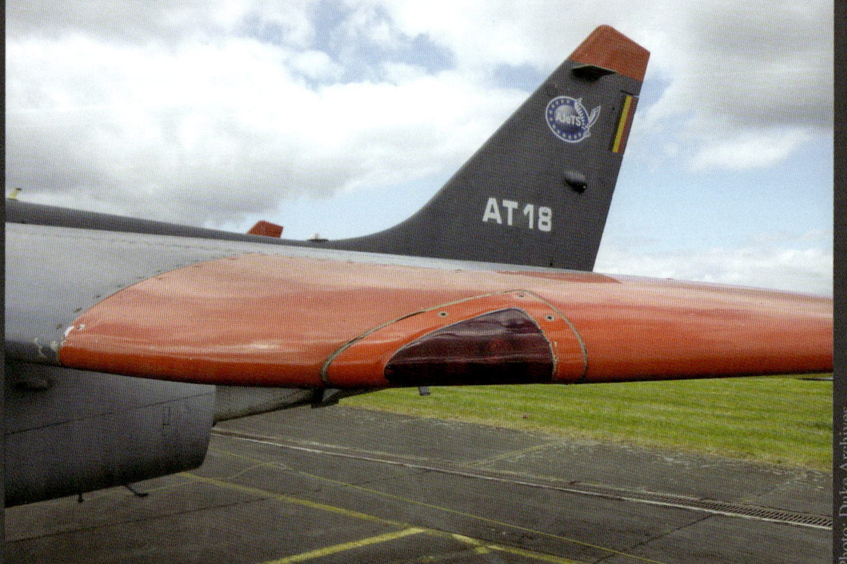

Above: On the forward part of the wing tip, a navigation light is located - red on the port side, green on the starboard side. Since it is a training jet, the wing tips are painted orange.

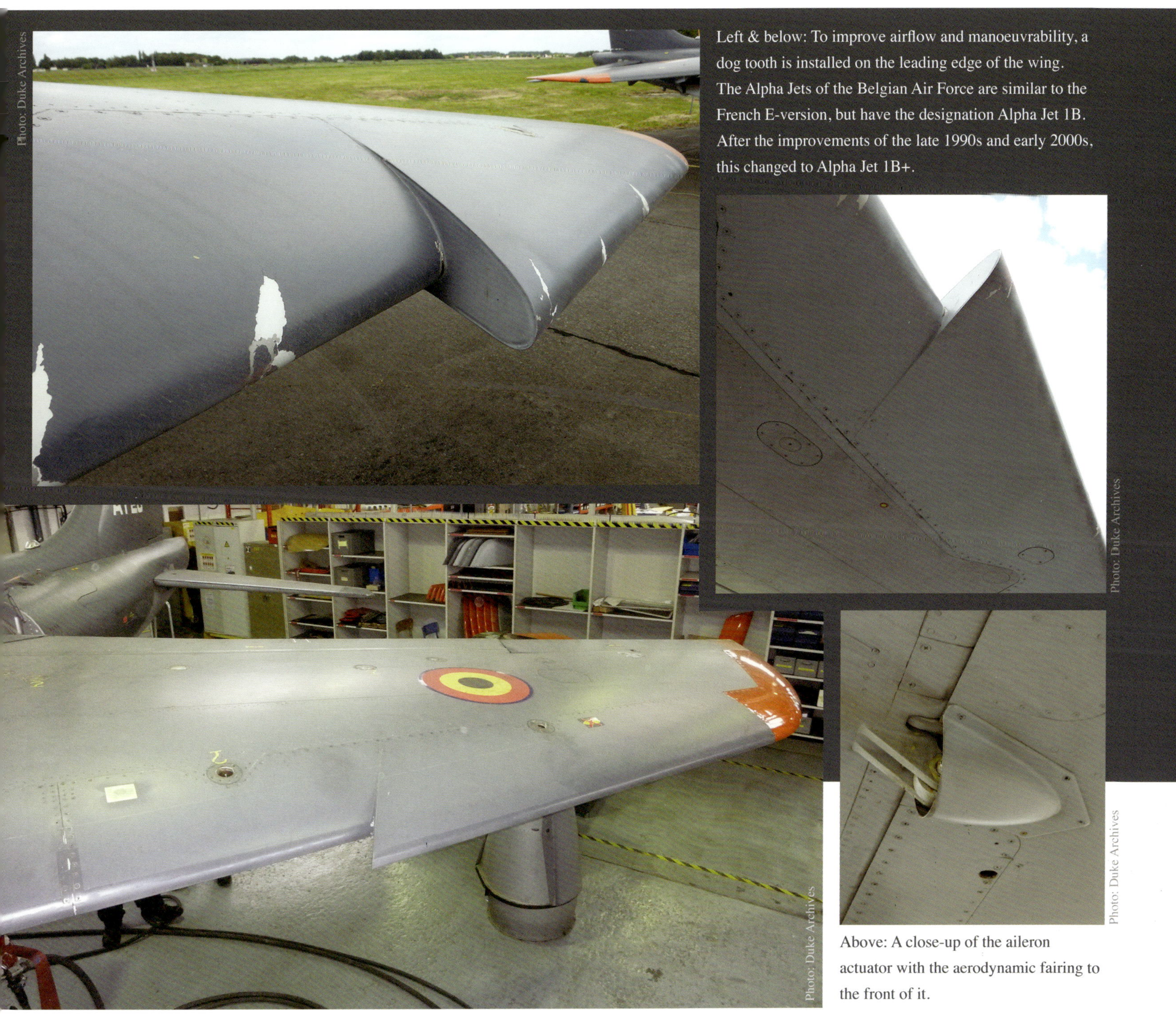

Left & below: To improve airflow and manoeuvrability, a dog tooth is installed on the leading edge of the wing. The Alpha Jets of the Belgian Air Force are similar to the French E-version, but have the designation Alpha Jet 1B. After the improvements of the late 1990s and early 2000s, this changed to Alpha Jet 1B+.

Photo: Duke Archives

Photo: Duke Archives

Photo: Duke Archives

Photo: Duke Archives

Above: A close-up of the aileron actuator with the aerodynamic fairing to the front of it.

With the Alpha Jet retiring from most air forces, the aircraft starts a second career with private companies. Here, a Gauntlet Aerospace Alpha Jet flies above the Mojave Desert in the summer of 2018. It is one of two Alpha Jets that are used as chase aircraft for test missions at Edwards. This jet is carrying a pair of external fuel tanks as well as some newly added antennas on the belly. The livery and decorations that were picked for this Alpha Jet, make the little jet look even faster!

Photo: Duke Archives

Photo: Duke Archives

Above & right: These photos show the triangular actuators for the trailing edge flaps. Speed and agility make that the Alpha Jet needs an impressive load-factor for such a small jet, ranging from + 8.6G to - 4G! The service ceiling of the aircraft is 48,000 feet, which can be reached with a speed of 57 meter per second.

A Belgian Alpha Jet 1B+ break away from a French Alpha Jet E over the Atlantic coast. Both aircraft are based at Cazaux, where the Franco-Belge AJets pilot school is located. Notice in this very cool shot the structure of the belly of the Alpha Jet and the oil spills on the aft fuselage. Look where the landing gear doors are located and the outwards position of the engine exhausts. The Belgian aircraft were painted in a two-tone grey finish, the French aircraft have a monochrome livery except for the black anti-glare part in front of the windscreen. Because all flight controls have servo-control, very fast and accurate flying can be obtained, very close to that of the fighter jets to which the student pilots hope to convert - The F-16 for the Belgian pilots, the Rafale or Mirage 2000 for their French classmates.

Photo: Robert Pied

Cockpit

These and the following pages show the cockpit of the Dassault/Dornier Alpha Jet, the first jet cockpit many current day fighter pilots sat in. Everything was designed to make it comfortable for the student-pilots: a clear lay-out of the instruments, good all-around view, easy access, ...
These photos show the final version of the Alpha Jet E and 1B+, which only differs slightly from the initial version. The two large dials in the center are the Altimeter on the right and the Airspeed Indicator on the left. The big black and yellow handle on the right, immediately above the warning panel, is the Emergency Parking Brake Handle.

Photo: Duke Archive

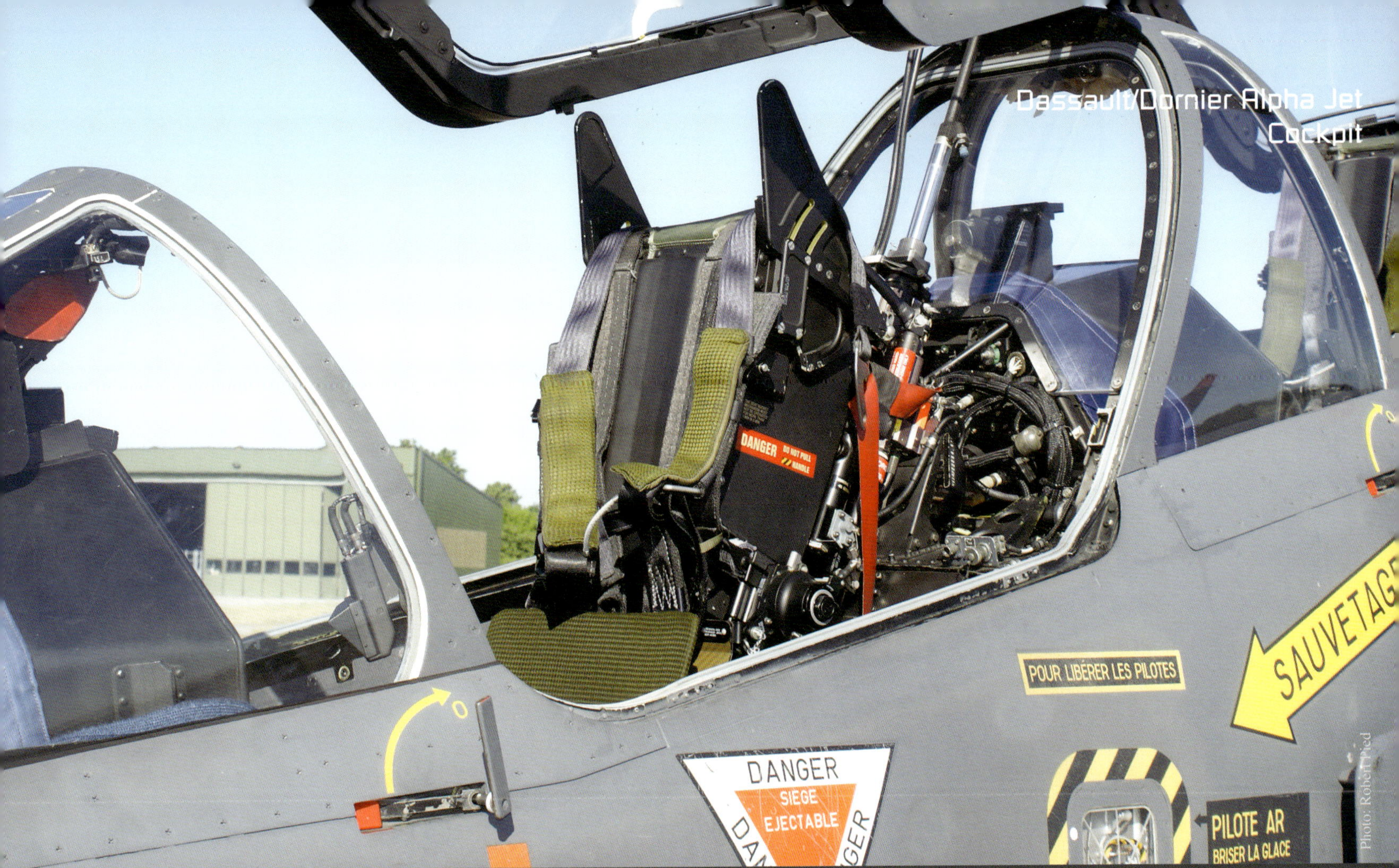

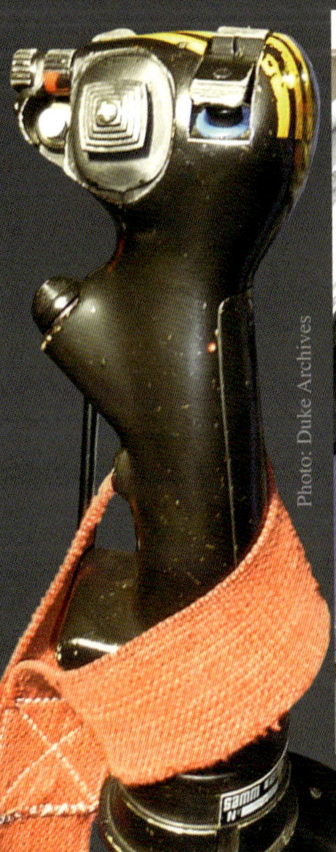

Above: A overall view of the forward cockpit of a French Alpha Jet with the Martin-Baker Mk.10N ejection seat. Prominent are the two large canopy breakers on top of the seat; the back seat has smaller ones. Notice the single actuator opening the canopy.

Right: The control stick of the Alpha Jet, with all the switches located on it.

Far Right: Initially, the Alpha Jet didn't have a HUD - Head-Up Display - but Belgium and France upgraded their aircraft in the 1990s and one of the modifications was the installation of a HUD in the front cockpit and a HUD repeater in the rear cockpit. Notice the stand-by compass on the windscreen framing.

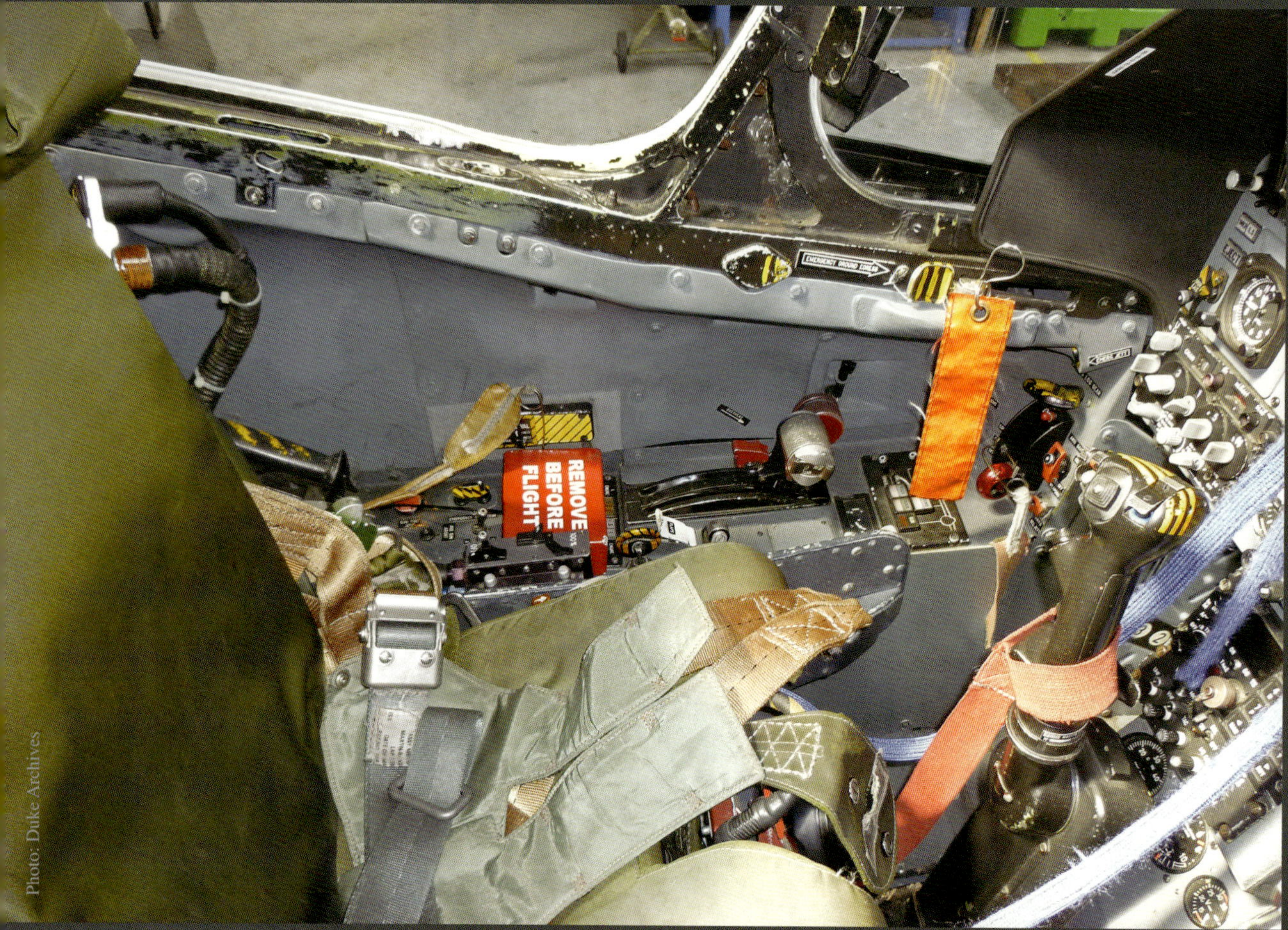

Left: The left hand console of the front cockpit with the Throttle as the most prominent part. The panel in front of it is the Armament Control panel. See the red wheel in the vertical black holder? That's the Landing Gear Control Handle, with the Gear Emergency Handle above it. To the left of it is the Landing Light switch. The black-and-yellow striped handle with the orange banner attached to it is the Canopy Severance Lever.

Below: Sitting in the cockpit, looking to the left, this is what you see. The tubing is of the anti-G system. In front of it are the Stabilator Emergency Trim Selector and the Starter panel. The sidewalls and instrument panels in the cockpit are all in medium grey.

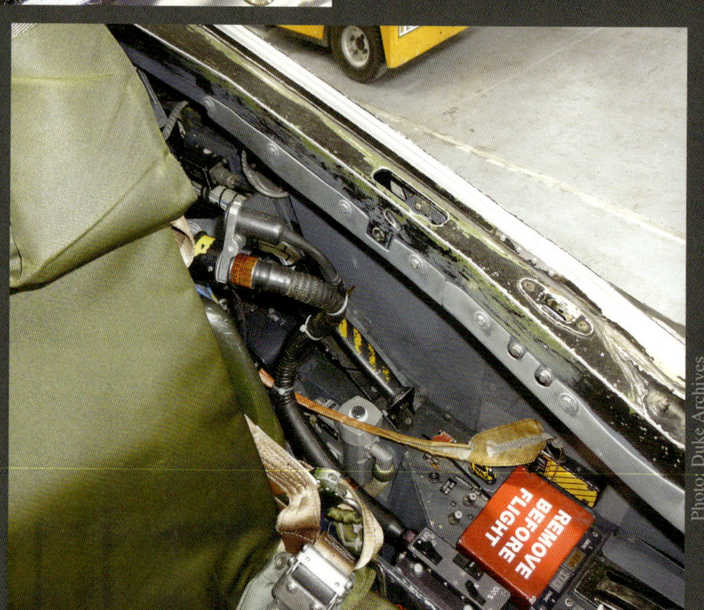

Photo: Robert Pied

Photo: Duke Archives

Above left: This photo shows the area behind the ejection seat, seen from the starboard side of the aircraft. Notice the glass windscreen seperating the two cockpits and the canopy actuator.

Above: The right hand side instrument console with most prominent the Emergency Parking Brake Handle. Below it is the Warning Light panel. To open or lock the canopy, the red handle has to be moved forward or backwards.

Left: The starboard side cockpit wall with the Defogging handle in the front and immediately behind it the blue RAM Air and Seal Inflation Control Lever. The tube to the right of the photo is the cockpit light. The black panel most aft on the console houses the Circuit Breakers.

Let's have a closer look at the backseat cockpit . This aircraft again, is the Belgian Alpha Jet 1B+, meaning that this is the updated version with the HUD Repeater prominent on the forward instrument panel. The dial on top of the instrument cover is the G-meter ranging from - 4 to +10. All instruments in the front cockpit are also available for the instructor in the back; the Emergency Brake handle to the right, stick in the middle and Throttle to the left. Similar to the front cockpit, a stand-by compass is fixed to the canopy framing. The quartet of dials on the right side of the instrument panel indicate information on the two engines: tachometers on top and tailpipe temperature below.

Below: The right hand side console which is as good as identical to the one in the front cockpit, except for the Defogging handle and the blue RAM Air and Seal Inflation Control Lever. The black switch panel in front of the control stick is the Intercom Control Box.

Photo: Robert Pied

Above: The ejection seat and the area behind it, seen from the starboard side. Look at all the connections to the rear bulckhead.

Below: The same area, seen from the port site of the aircraft.

Photo: Robert Pied

Photo: Robert Pied

Above: This photo shows the same area, but this time, the aircraft is of the Armée de l'Air. Notice that the ejection seat is painted black. Look at all the details of the canopy framing.

Above: Another close-up of the aft instrument panel. The dial on top to the right is the Hydraulic Pressure Indicator. The yellow square next to it is the Fail Light and below that the Fuel Tank Warning Lights, with the red one in the centre lighting up at 250 liter. Notice the rudder pedal behind the panel.

Left & above left: The left hand side of the back seat cockpit - again, compare it to the front seat cockpit on page 40. Look at the throttle and the deep red handles of it. The grey switch on the throttle itself is the Speed Brake selector.

Above: The flight control stick of the aft cockpit.
Look at the Airspeed indicator, Altimeter,
Artificial Horizon and the Navigation indicator
behind it.

Right: To the left are the switches of the UHF
Control Box and the Ejection Command switch.

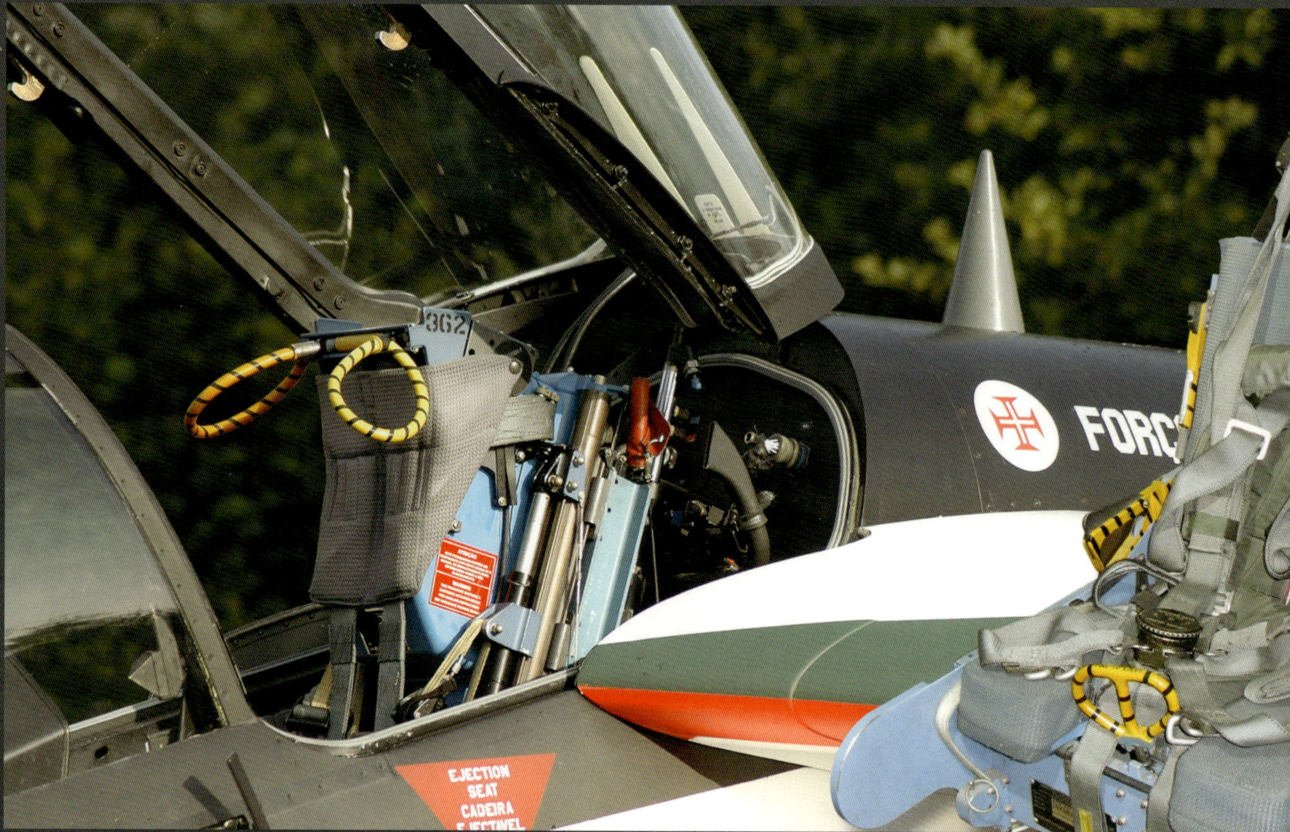

Photo: Jens Schymura

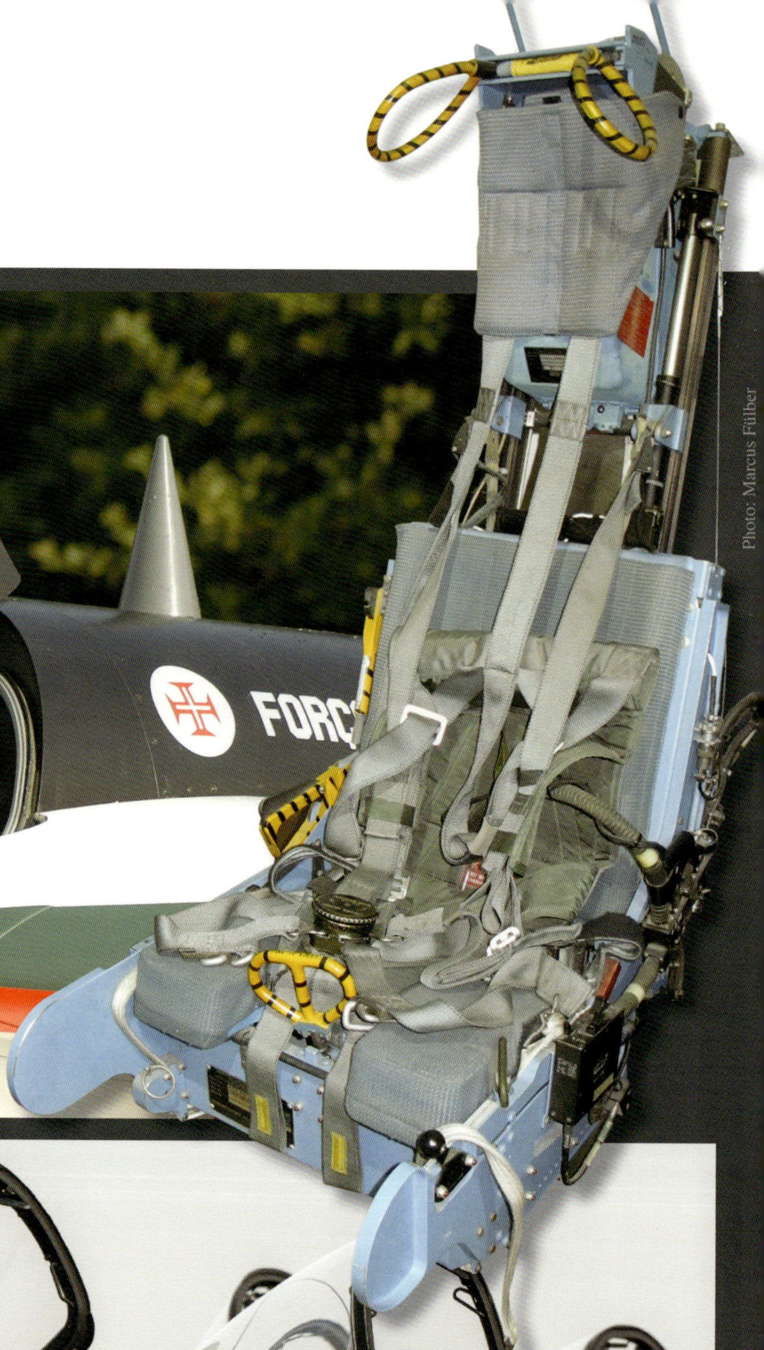

Photo: Marcus Fülber

Three types of ejection seats can be found in the cockpit of the Alpha Jet; on this page is the Stencil ejection seat, that was installed in the German aircraft - and thus also the Portuguese ones, since they are former Luftwaffe aircraft. Initially, the French Alpha Jet E was equipped with the Martin-Baker MK.4 ejection seat.

The Stencil ejection seat that was used had a distinctive light blue finish and two overhead ejection handles. The French used the Mk.4 - see page 37 - which is a zero-ninety seat, meaning that it can only be used at speeds in excess of 90 knots - 167 km/h. Look at the details in these photos of the Stencil seat and the differences between the front seat and the backseat. The seat, head rest and the straps are light grey, the seat itself is in light blue.

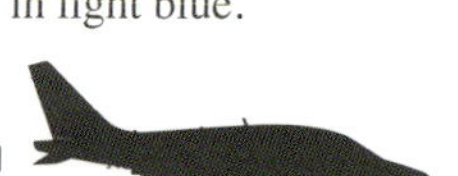

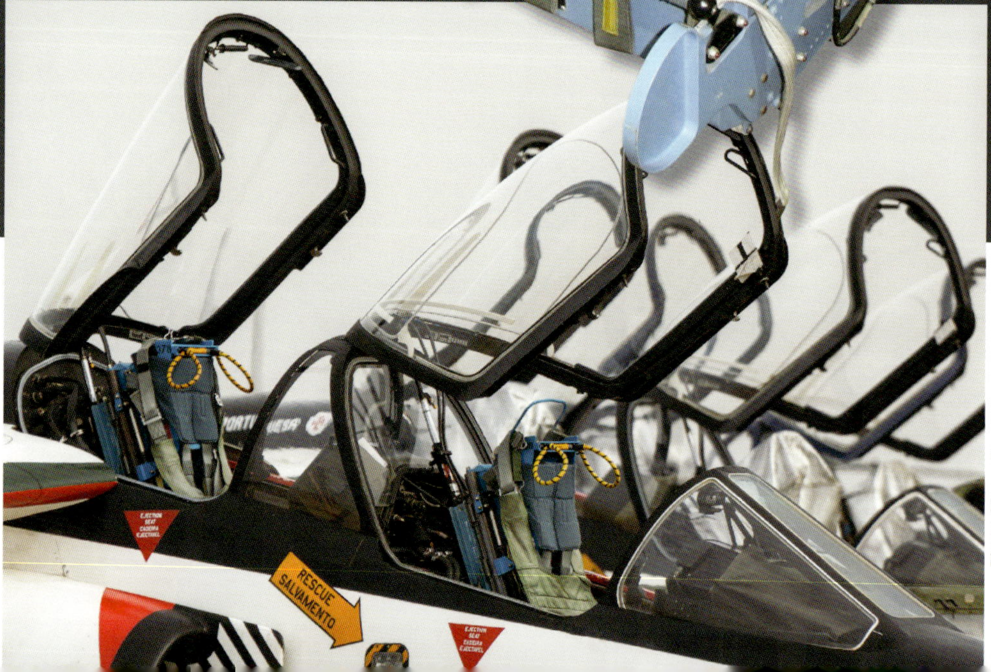

Photo: Marco Casaleiro

Martin-Baker Mk.10

These photos show the Martin-Baker Mk.10 ejection seat as they were installed in the Alpha Jets of the Belgian Air Force. This, to be exact, is a backseat ejection seat, which can be recognised by the small canopy breakes on top of the seat. Look at page 39 to compare with the front seat. The big advantage of the Mk.10 over the Mk.4 is that it is a fully automated zero-zero ejection seat that can be used at any altitude to bring the crew to safety in case of an emergency. The seat is designed in 4 main units: the catapult, the main beam structure, the seat pan and finally the parachute assembly. Because of these sub-structures, it is possible to quickly install or remove the seat. The Martin-Baker Mk.10 proved to be a highly reliable seat and over 5,000 of them were produced. Variants of this seat can also be found in aircraft such as the Mirage 2000, Panavia Tornado, Hawk or Saab Gripen. When the crew finds itself in a situation where it has to eject, they pull the ring in front of them. 0.25 seconds later, the rocket ignites and emergency oxygen is activated. At 0.5 seconds after firing, the rocket engine burns out and the drogue gun fires. 1 second later, the parachute is deployed and the seat and pilot are seperated. When the chute is fully deployed, the locator beacon is activated and rescue teams can start looking for the crew...

Photo: Robert Pied

Photo: Robert Pied

Photo: Philip Stevens

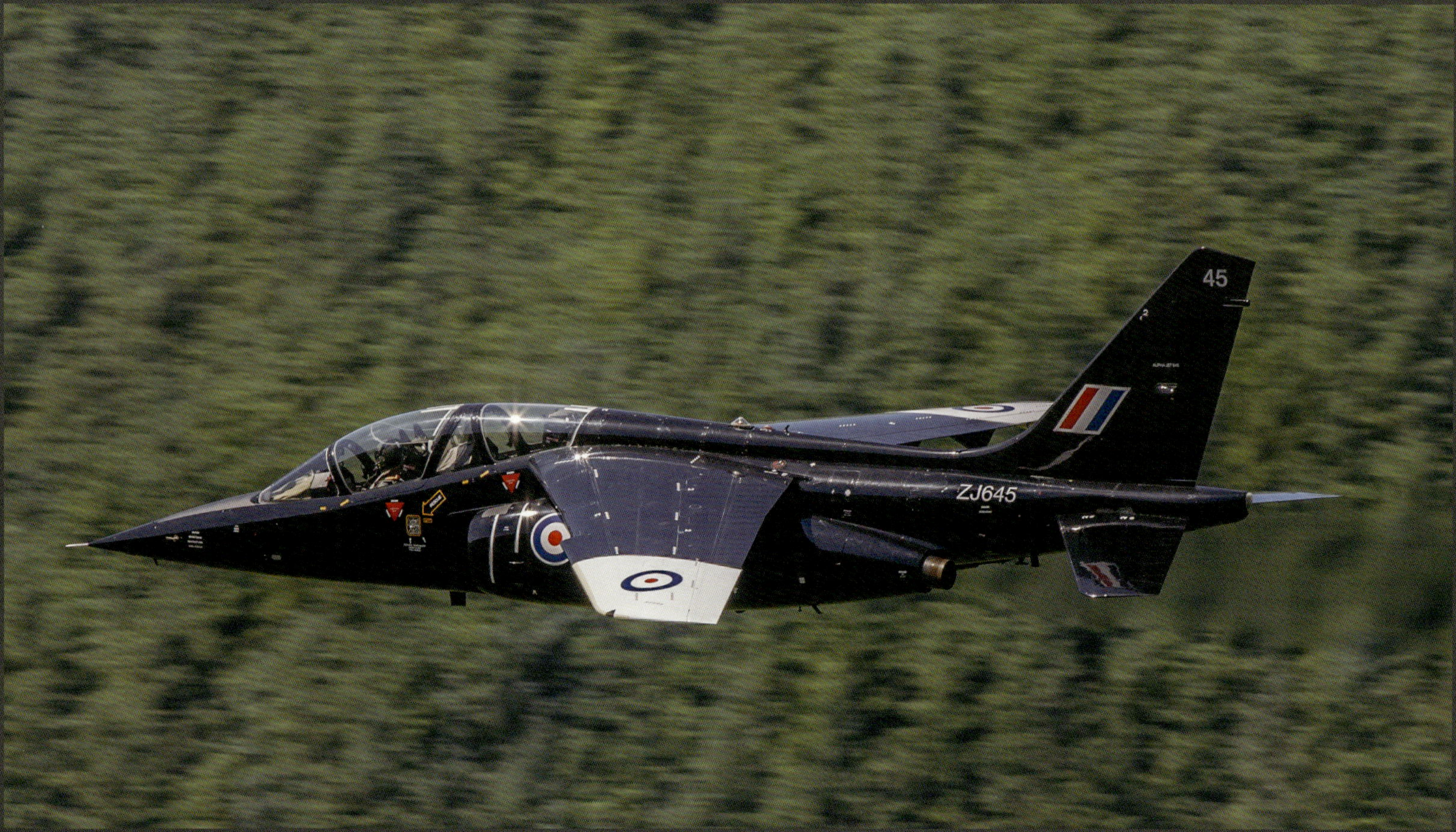

UK based Alpha Jets

For many air forces and private companies, the former Luftwaffe Alpha Jet As have been a source of aircraft. Portugal and Thailand bought quite a few and Canada's Top Aces is operating a large number in very cool liveries. In the UK, QinetiQ bought a dozen of them in the late 1990s as successors to the Hawks that it had in its fleet, but were required to re-join the RAF. Six of them were operated as part of the Empire Test Pilots' School. The photo above shows one of them zipping through the Mach Loop in Wales, the one to the right in the static of the Air Tattoo. The aircraft were withdrawn from use in 2018 and .... sold to Top Aces.

Photo: Peter Anthoni

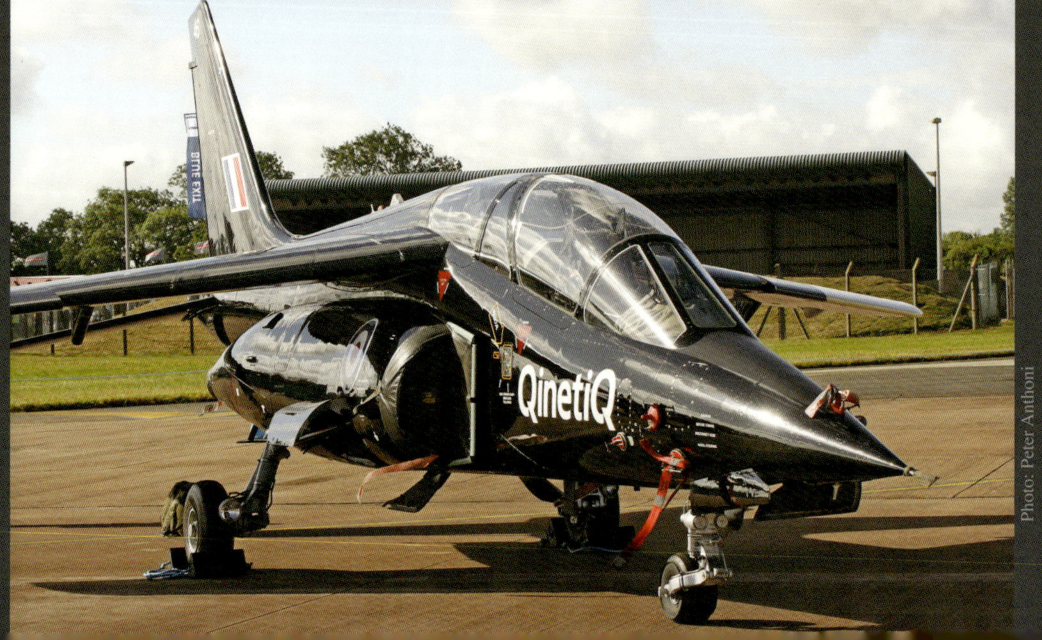

Photo: Philip Stevens

Photo: Adrian Pingstone

Left: The Empire Test Pilot School - what they do is clearly in the name - is run under a partnering arrangement between the UK MoD and QinetiQ, which also uses the Alpha Jet for exercises in performance, stability and control and flying qualities. The Alpha Jets are former German Air Force aircraft and are based at Boscombe Down.

Here, ZJ646 is seen at RIAT and taxies after landing to its parking spot in the Static Display.

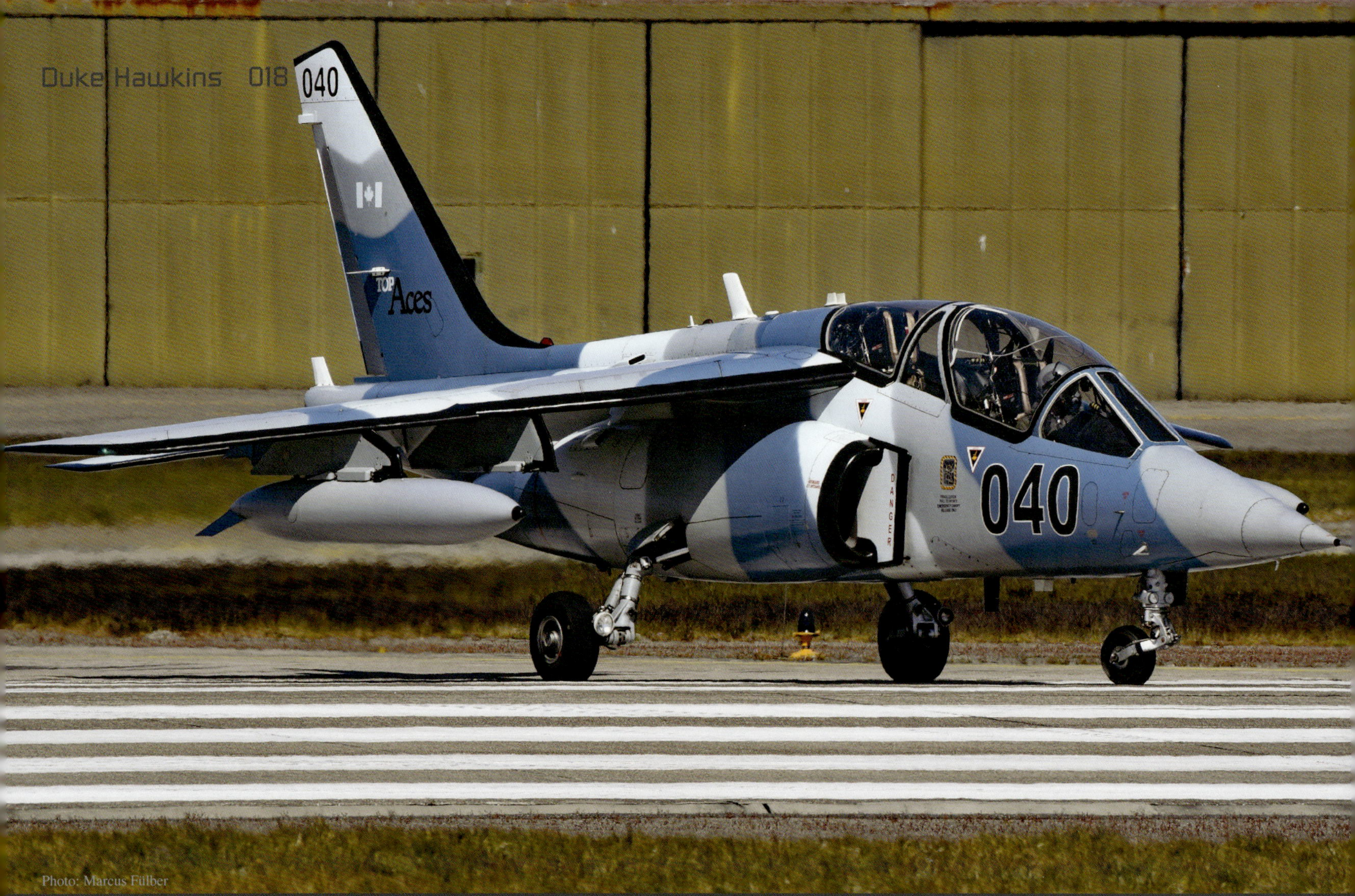

Photo: Marcus Fülber

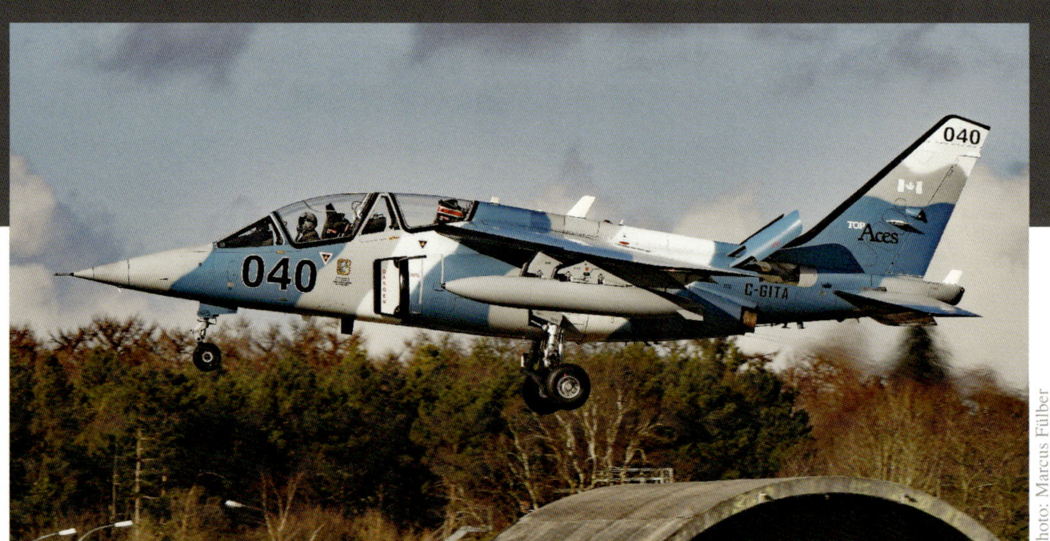

Adversary Alpha Jet

With it's speed and agility, the Alpha Jet is a cheap and able jet to be used as an adversary aircraft by private companies. Top Aces, based in Wittmund, northern Germany, mostly flies the A-4N Skyhawk, with the Alpha Jet as a good alternative. These photos show some of the aircraft that are used by the company in the adversary role. Not only are they painted in some very cool liveries, they have been upgraded with some specific equipment. Look at the large white blade antennas on the spine and aft of the vertical tail and on the fin itself. Typical are also the double antenna and gps receiver, aft of the cockpit.

Photo: Marcus Fülber

Right: A Top Aces Alpha Jet A is returning after a flight. Notice the different style antennas on the back of the aircraft, the open speed brakes and the underwing pylons. See the red circle on the base of the wing, near the trailing edge? This is the gravity refuelling point. This photo to me actually demonstrates to good effect the clean lines of the Alpha Jet. Notice that the Stencil ejection seat has been replaced by a more modern one.

Photo: Marcus Fülber

Photo: Marcus Fülber

Above: 069 is coming in after a flight and has its speed brakes deployed. Sporting a pretty cool camouflage, this Alpha Jet is being used in the adversary role. Notice that the aft ejection seat isn't installed and that the aircraft is carrying a pair of external fuel tanks. The Canadian company must be quite satisfied with the performance of the Alpha Jet, since it purchased some 25 of the type from the Belgian Air Force, that retired its jets in 2018.

Photo: Marcus Fülber

Landing the Alpha Jet

The Alpha Jet has a typical tricycle landing gear, with widely placed main gear struts, making sure that pilots have a comfortable and stable landing. The front landing gear is off set to starboard to make room for the gun, so that even with the gear down, the gun can be operated.

Left: This head-on shot of a Portuguese Alpha Jet shows to good effect how the nose wheel is positioned to the starboard side of the aircraft, to give room for the gun nozzle in the pod underneath the fuselage.

Photo: Marco Casaleiro

Photo: Kris Christiaens

Photo: Jens Schymura

Photo: Guillaume Friart

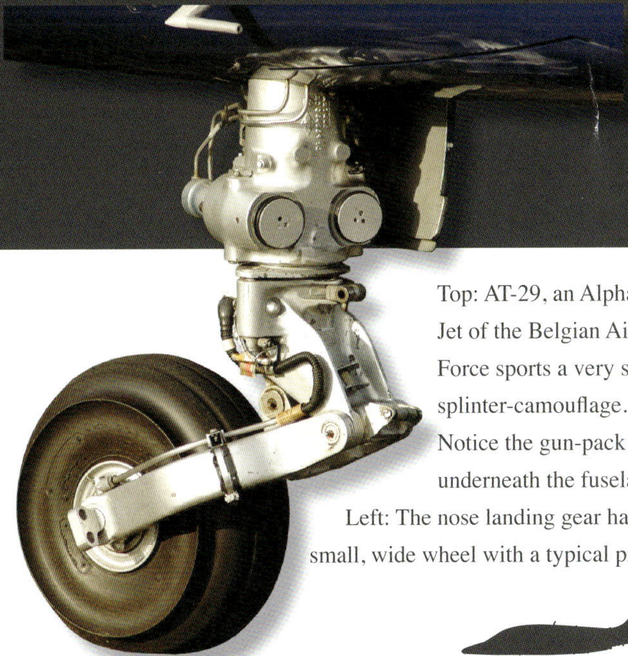

Top: AT-29, an Alpha Jet of the Belgian Air Force sports a very smart splinter-camouflage. Notice the gun-pack underneath the fuselage.

Left: The nose landing gear has a small, wide wheel with a typical profile.

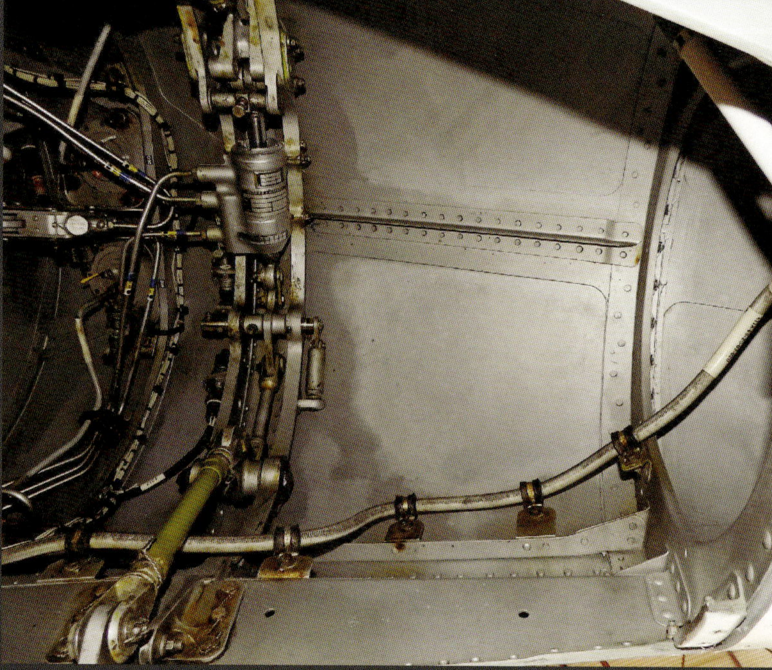

These photos show the forward landing gear bay of the Alpha Jet. Notice the green bars of the landing gear door actuators and all the wiring running through the bay. The interior of the bay has a metal finish; the wheel folds forward into the bay when the pilot brings up the gear lever on the left hand console.

Photo: Robert Pied

Photo: Peter Anthoni

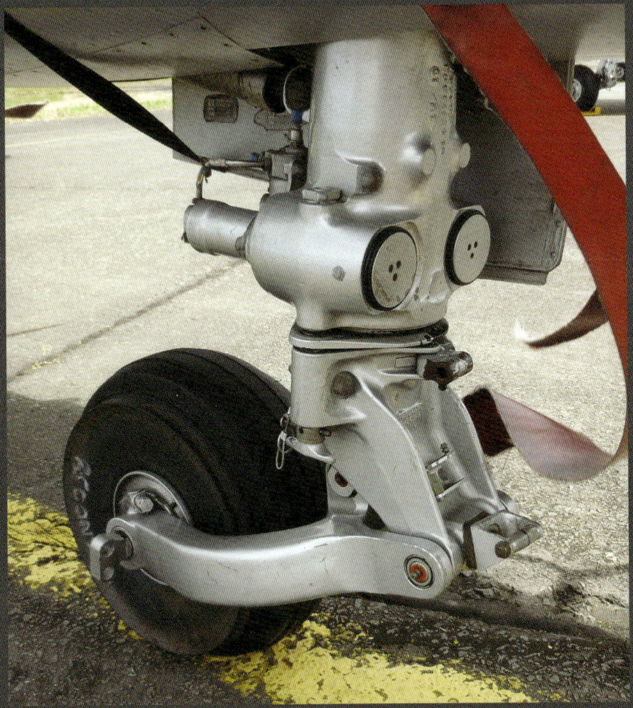

Photo: Duke Archives

Above: The nose wheel with the gear door attached to it. Before each flight, the tires have to be checked by ground crew and pilots, especially the depth of the grooves in the tires. If there is any doubt about the status, they are replaced.

Photo: Robert Pied

Below: A good close-up of the front gear bay, looking aft. Look at where the gear strut is fixed to the fuselage. The landing speed of the aircraft is 170 km/h and it takes the aircraft some 500 meters to come to a full stop after touch-down.

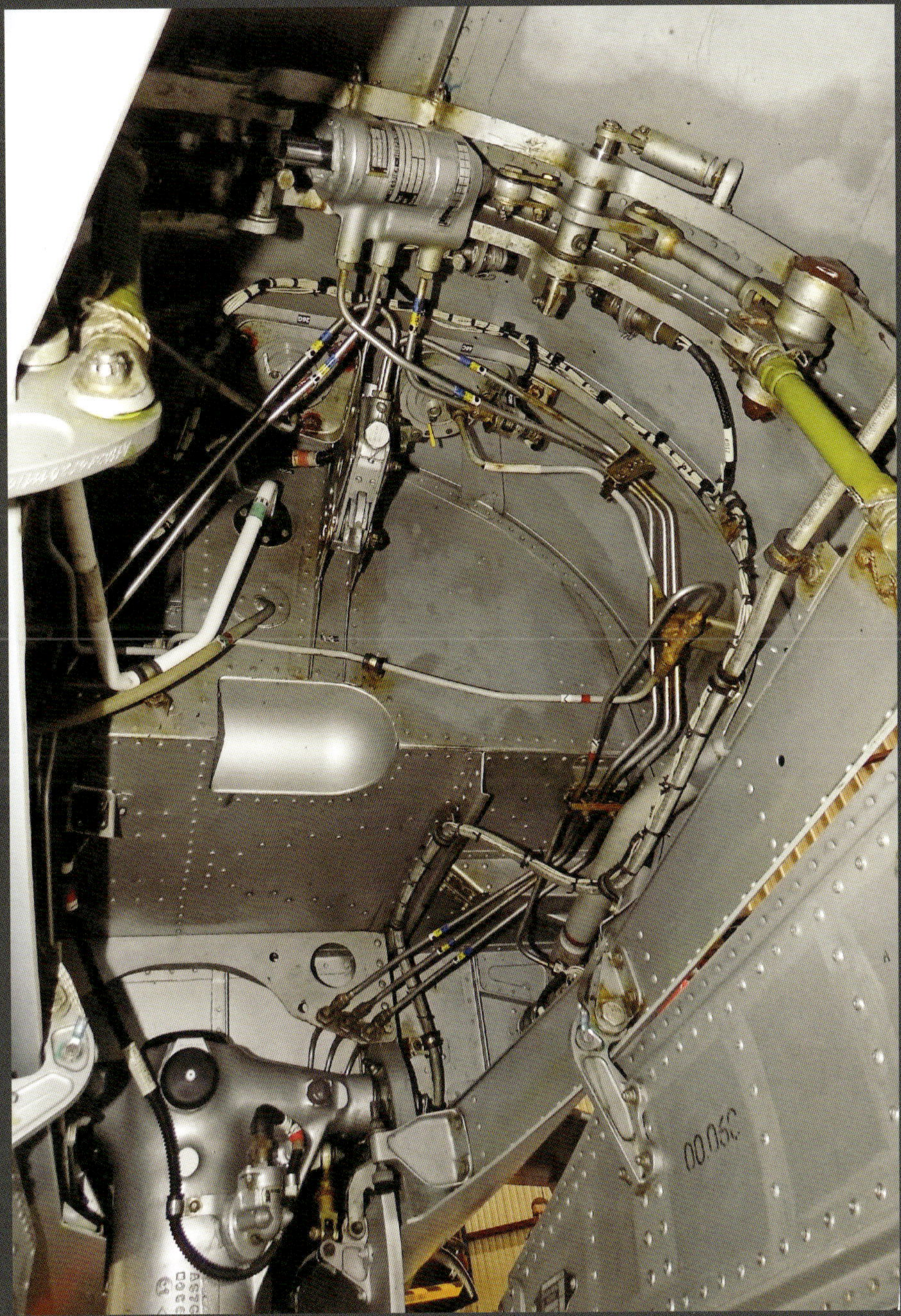

Photo: Robert Pied

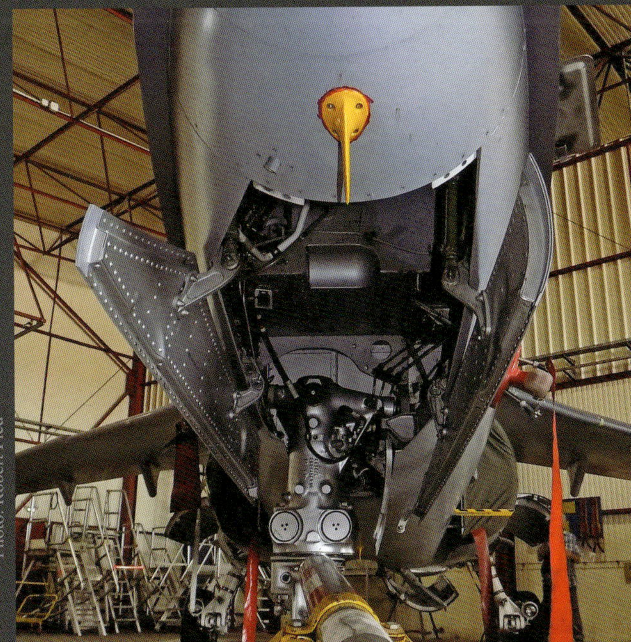

Photo: Philip Stevens

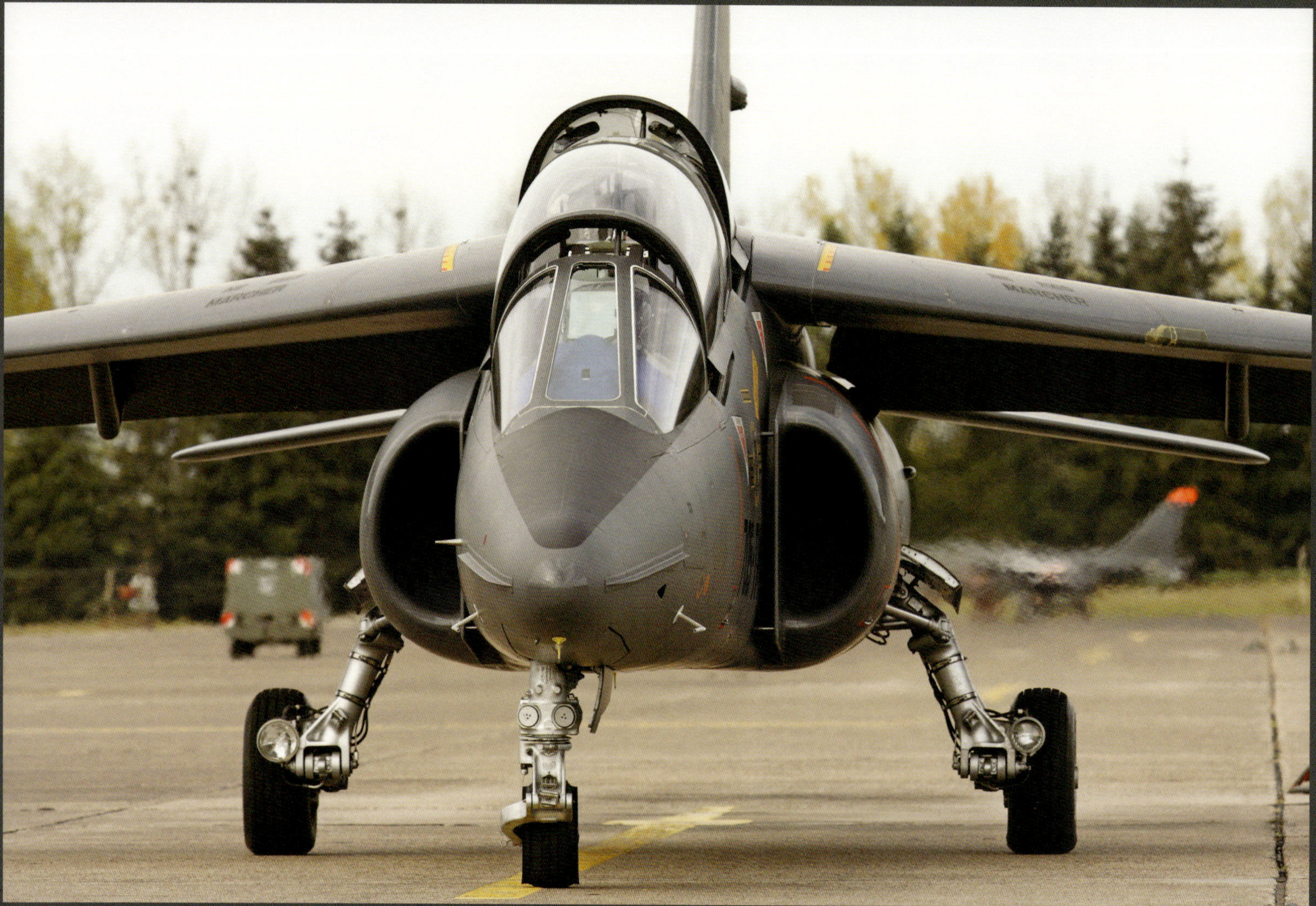

Above: Looking from this angle, with the flaps down, the Alpha Jet looks pretty cool, I think. Look how wide the track is of the main landing gear. The French Alpha Jets have an Angle of Attack probe on the starboard side of the nose, which the Belgian 1B+ aircraft don't have.

Right: A close-up of the forward gear strut and the actuator attached to it. Look at the connections and the details of the inside of the nose gear door.

Photo: Guillaume Friart

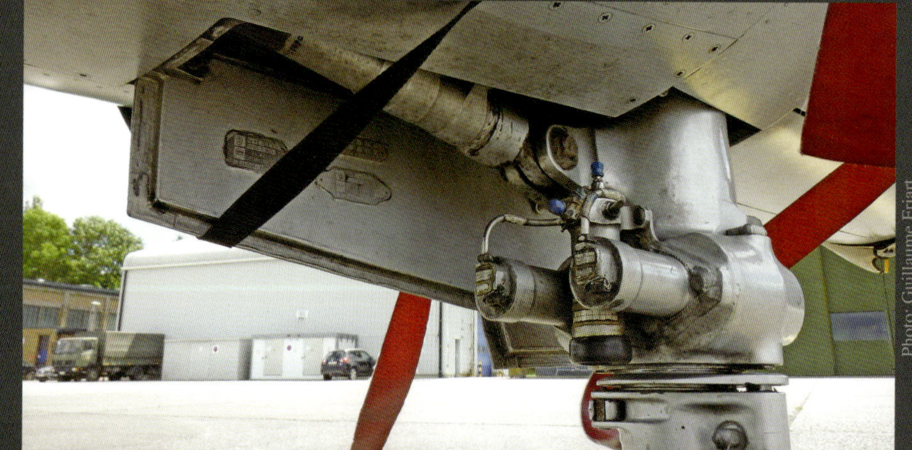

Photo: Marco Casaleiro

This Asas de Portugal Alpha Jet is just seconds into the air and is in the process of retracting the landing gear. Both nose and main gear is folding forward, with the wheels of the latter turning 90 degrees into the wheel bays.

Photo: Robert Pied

Photo: Peter Anthoni

Above: This Alpha Jet of the Patrouille de France is in it's finals before touch-down and has the speed brakes out and the trailing edge flaps down. Notice how the nosewheel is fully extended.
Left: The typical profile of the small, but wide nose wheel and the actuator pushing the gear above it.

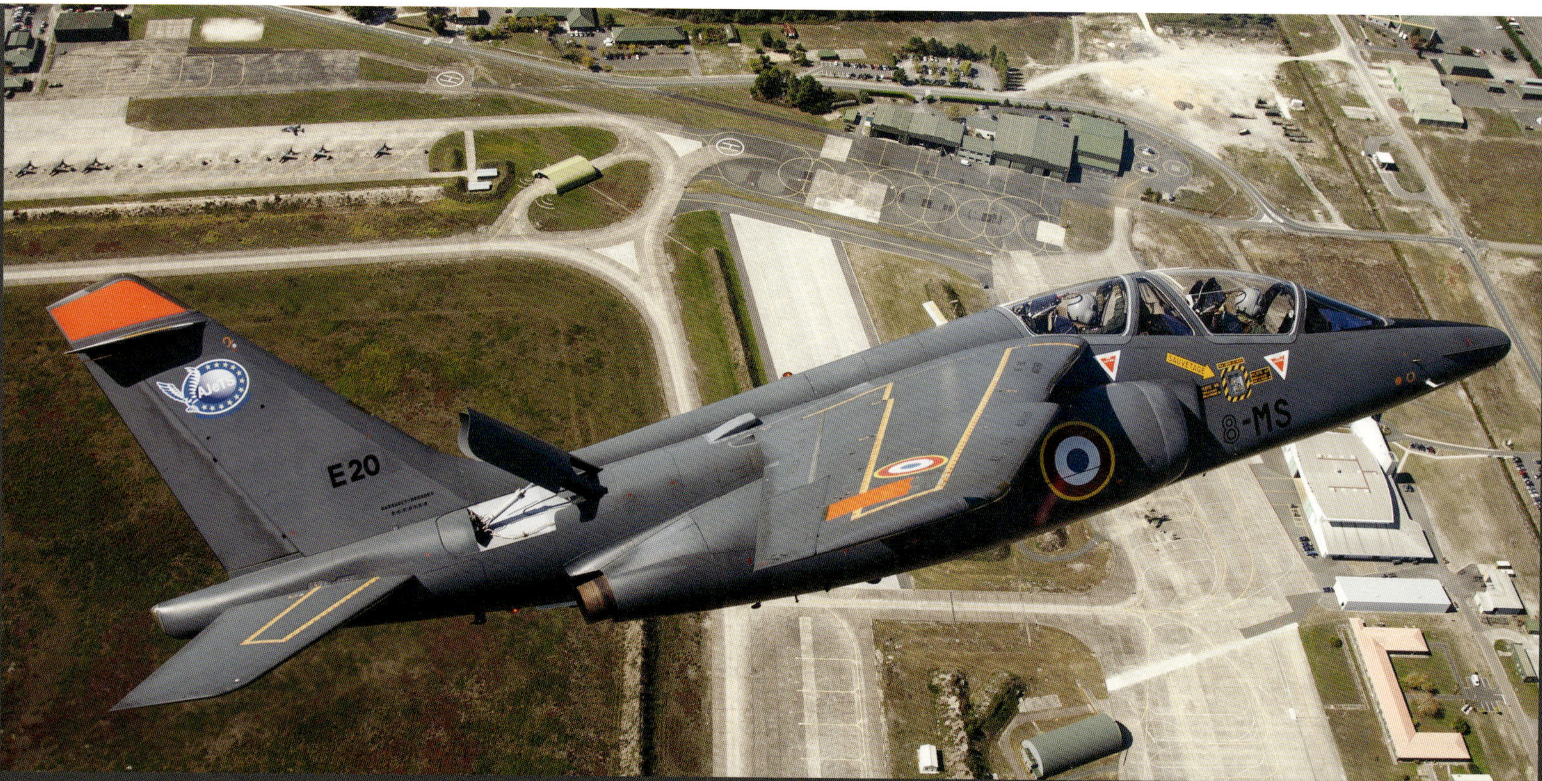

Photo: Sirpa

Photo: Jens Schymura

Photo: Jens Schymura

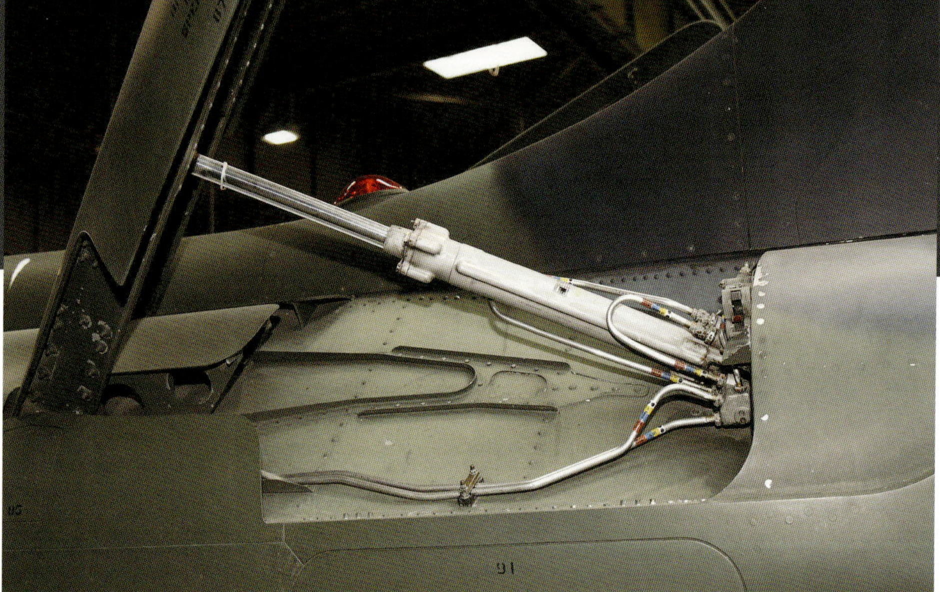

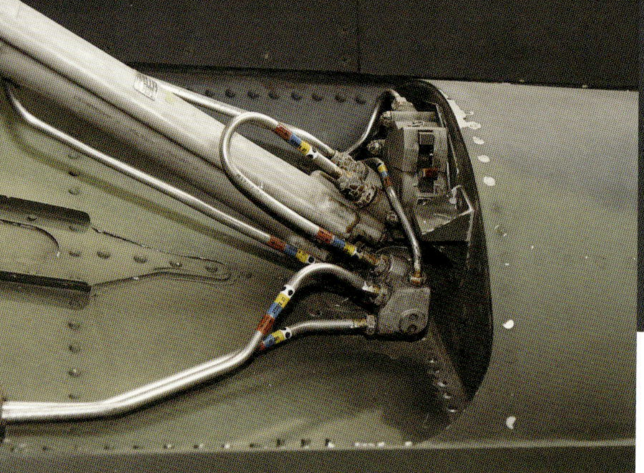

The Alpha Jet has a pair of large speed brakes located on the top of the aft fuselage. The stall speed of the aircraft with the flaps and gear down is 167 km/h, in flight with the gear and flaps up, the Alpha Jet starts to stall at a speed of 216 km/h. The top photo shows a French AJets flying over Cazaux.

Left and below: The open speed brake in closer detail. Each speed brake is moved by a single hydraulically operated actuator. Notice the internal structure of the door and the lines running along the base .

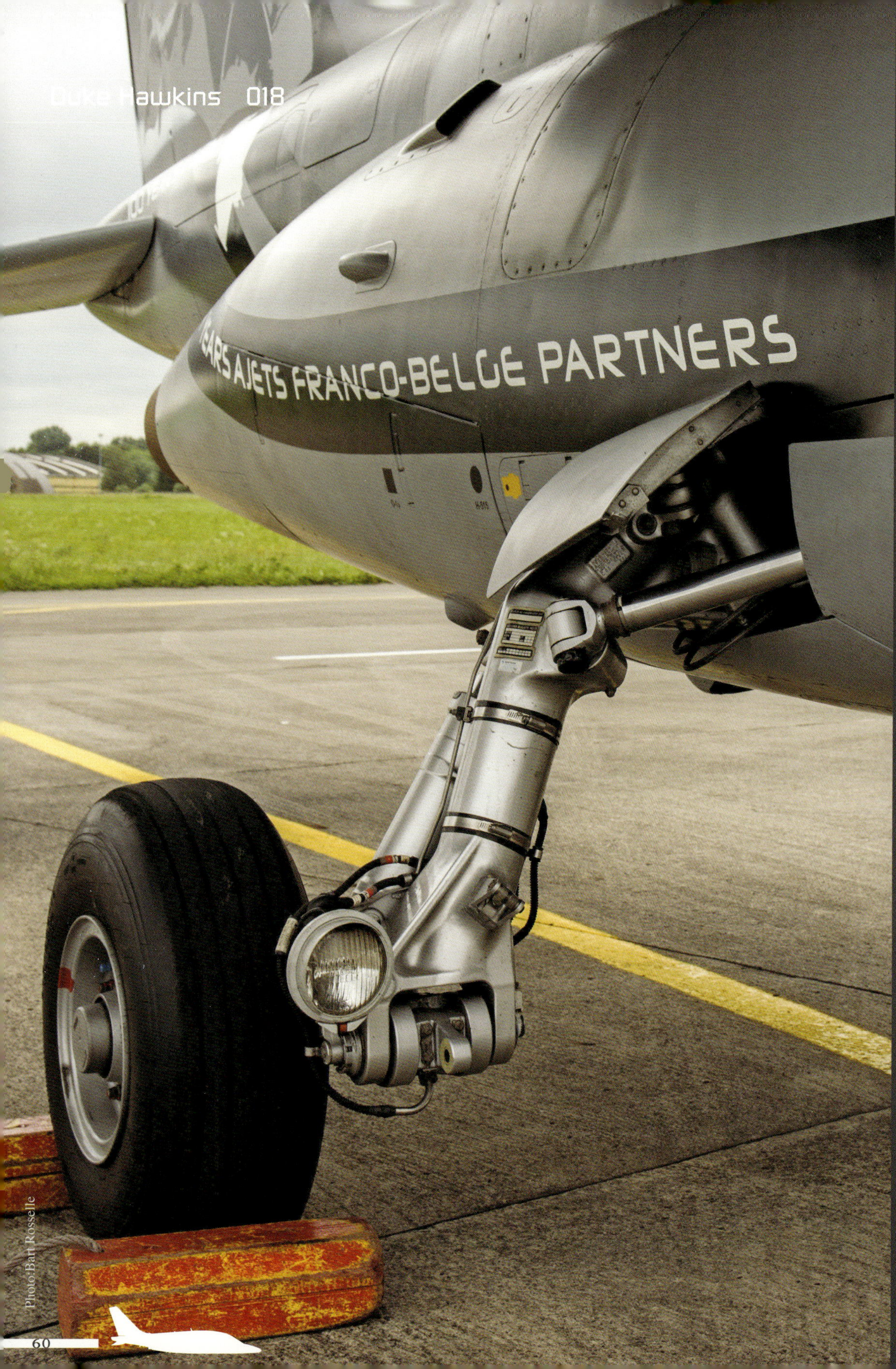

The main landing gear of the Alpha Jet is wide to give the aircraft stable handling characteristics during landing and taxiing. Each gear has a large wide wheel with a landing light fixed to it. The gear has three landing gear doors, of which the two large ones are always closed on the ground - they only open when the gear is being retracted or lowered. Upon retracting, an actuator pulls the gear forward into the wheel bays. The struts are painted white or metal.

Photo: Jens Schymura

Above: The starboard landing gear and wheel bay of a Portuguese Alpha Jet. Notice the large actuator, pushing the main gear out or pulling it in.
Far right: the starboard main gear seen from above. Right: On the outside of each main landing gear struts, a landing light is located.

Photo: Duke Archives

Photo: Robert Pied

Landing the Alpha Jet

These photos show the main gear in close detail. Notice the tie-down point in orange at the back of the gear and the structure on the inside of the wheels. The gear consists of 4 major parts: the main strut and the strut to which the wheel is connected, a third strut connecting both of them and the actuator that pushes the gear forward into the wheel well on take-off and back out during landing. Most of the lines running over the gear are located at the back of the main strut, with electrical wires in a black protection tube for the landing light. The switch to engage the landing lights is located on the left side of the instrument panel, next to the landing gear lever. Depending on the brand of the tires, inspection before each flight is slightly different. Each tire is carefully checked for cuts or wear and tear on all sides.

Photo: Duke Archives

Photo: Robert Pied

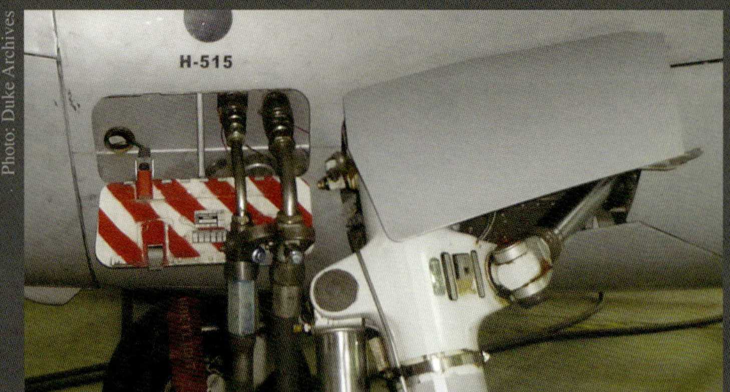

Above & right: The small landing gear door of the starboard main gear and the access door aft of it. The photo below shows an Alpha Jet on jacks, with the gear fully extended and a brand new wheel installed.

Above: A Goodyear tire and the braking mechanisme on the inside of it in close detail. Notice the connection between the main and lower struts and the wiring running over them.

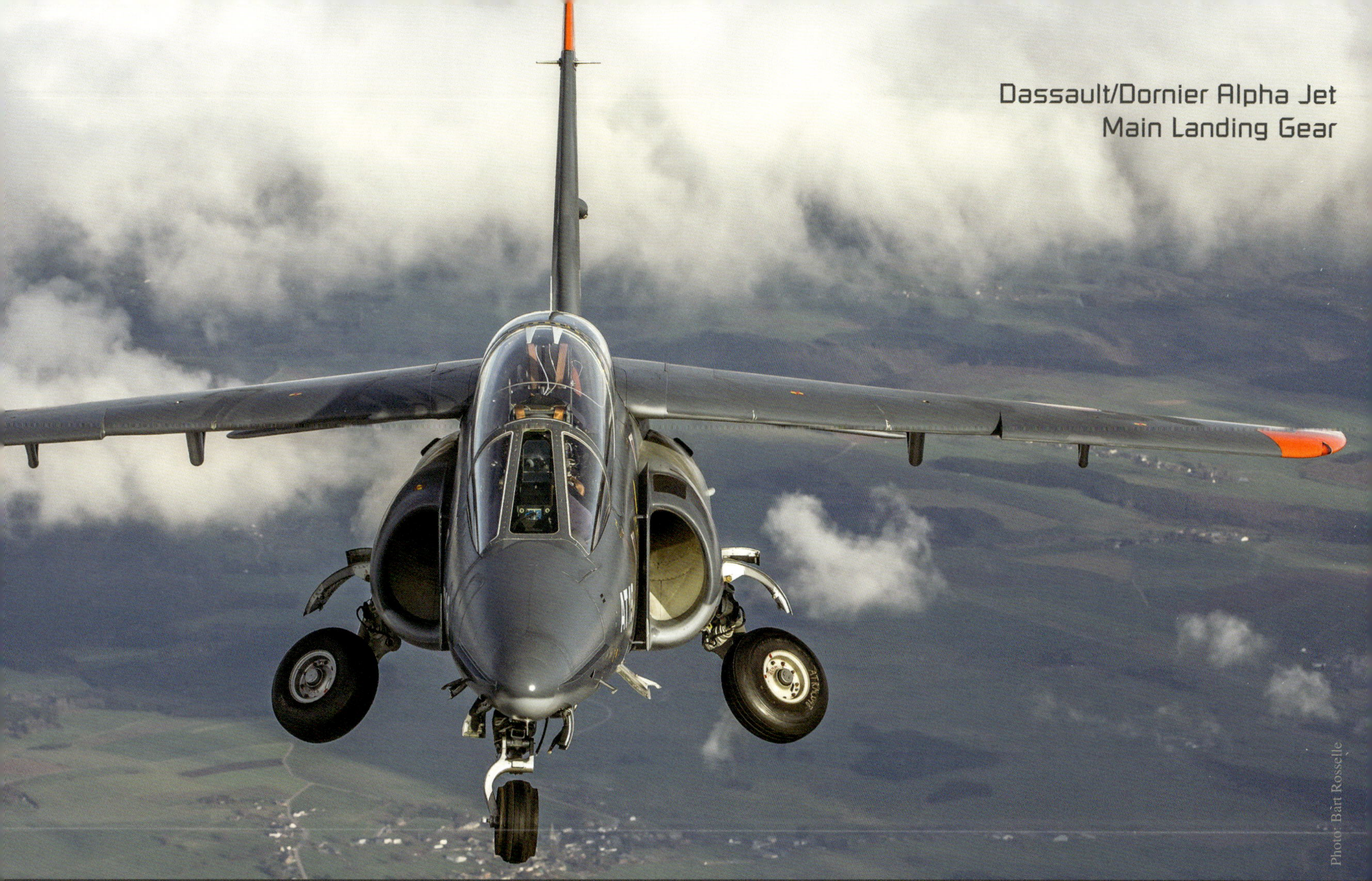

Photo: Bart Rosselle

Above: A Belgian Air Force Alpha Jet 1B+ is lowering the landing gear in flight. Look how they all fold forward and how the gear doors are activated. The main gear wheels turns more inwards at the last moment to fit into the bays.

Right: The port main landing gear, looking aft. Look at the position of the landing light.

Far right: The same wheel, but this time seen from above and aft. Notice the red tie-down point.

Photo: Guillaume Friart

Photo: Duke Archives

Photo: Robert Pied

Except for when the gear is retracting or lowered, the two large main gear doors are opened, but that isn't a reason not to give you a look inside the wheel bays. These photos were taken when some aircraft were in maintenance. The main gear bays have a metal finish and are cramped with pipes and wires on the inside wall. The photo above is of the port wheel bay looking aft, with the actuators linked to the white painted gear. Notice the hinges of the upper bay door and the black covered electrical lines. The gear door actuators have green painted struts.

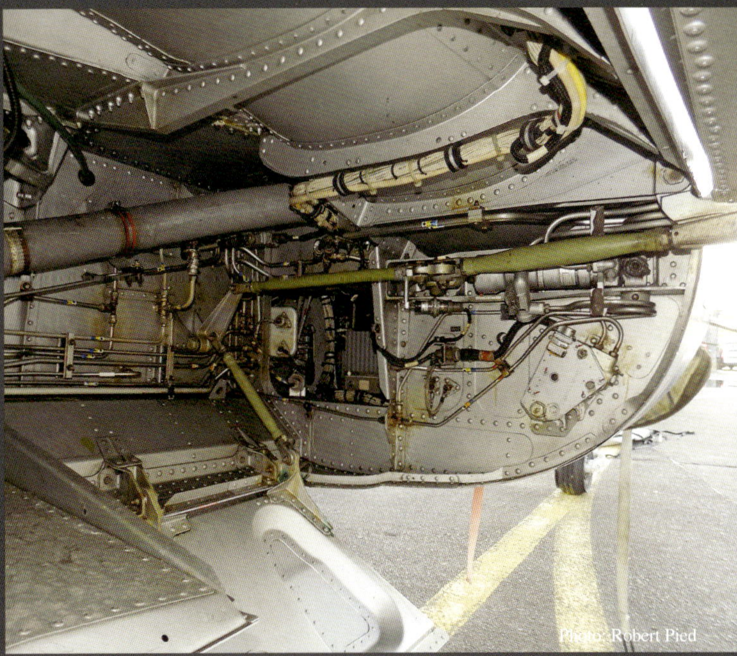

These photos show the starboard main landing gear bay in every detail. On the ground, the two large landing gear doors are usually closed, so these details will be invisible, except for when the jet is in maintenance.

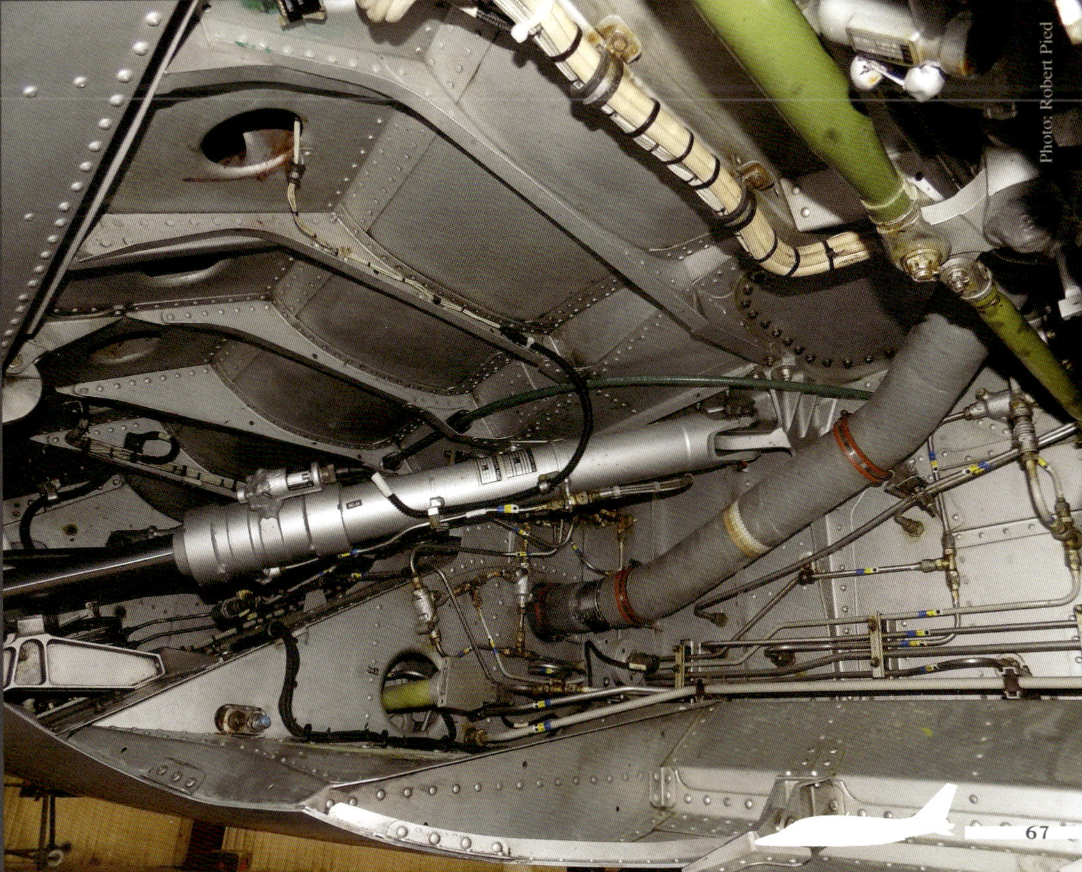

Above: The base of the small main landing gear door on the starboard side, looking forward. Below: The port main gear looking forward. Look how far the wheel stands outside of the fuselage.

Above: The forward main gear door on the port side lowered and in close-up.

Opposite page top: AT-24 was the last Belgian Air Force Alpha Jet to get a special livery. The occasion was the 40th anniversary of the type in service with the Belgian Air Force, but also the 100th anniversary of 11 Squadron. The unit, which used to be a night-fighter unit when it flew jets like the Meteor NF11 or the CF-100 Canuck has a bat as the unit logo, hence the large stylised bat on the vertical tail. Being part of the Franco-Belge AJets, the port side carried a Belgian flag on the horizontal tail and the top view of an F-16, while the port side carried a French flag and a Rafale.

Photo: Bart Rosselle

Photo: Duke Archives

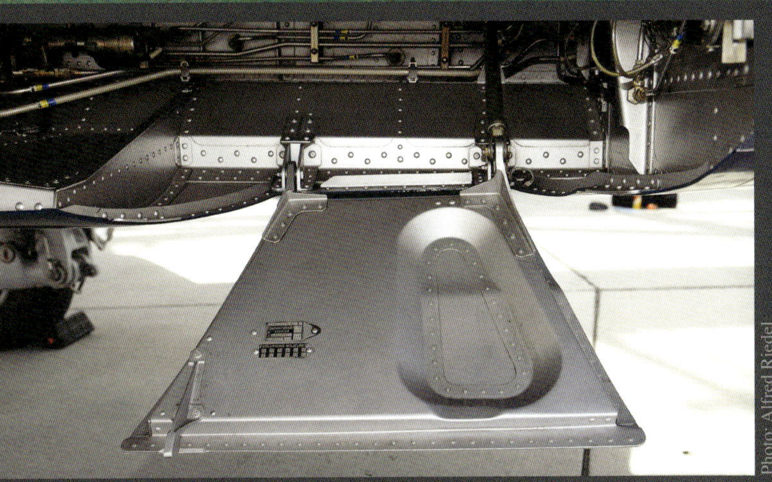

Photo: Alfred Riedel

Photo: Bart Rosselle

Photo: Peter Anthoni

The tip of the vertical tail stands at 4,19 meter with the tip - in the photo above painted in dayglo-orange - housing the VHF/UHF radio antenna and TACAN antenna. Below it, on either side, is the VOR antenna blade. AT-22, the Alpha Jet braking away to the left, carries an SUU20A rocket and bomb dispenser, loaded with 4 blue practice bombs on the port side and a DEFA 30 mm gun pod on the centerline.

Left: AT-11, another Alpha Jet 1B+ returns from a training flight. Look at the rudder, which has a single actuator on the port side. This aircraft too has the gun pod installed.

Photo: Robert Pied

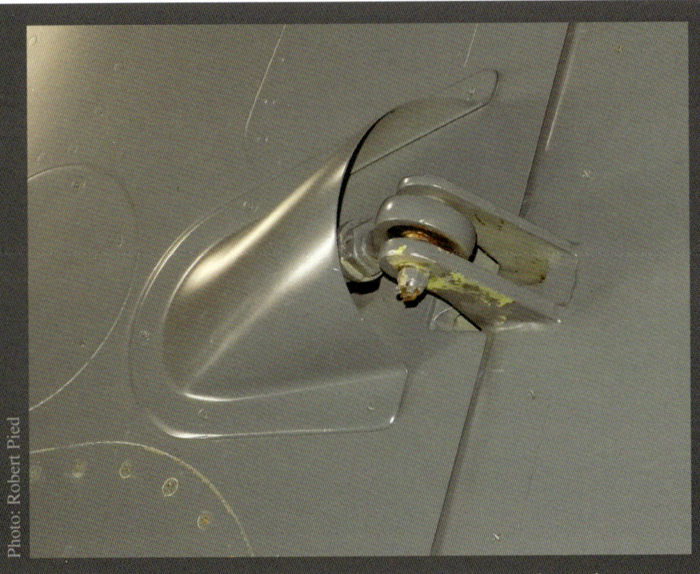

Above: A close-up of the rudder actuator and the aerodynamic cover over it, which is located on the port side of the vertical tail.

Below: The structure of the vertical tail with the VOR blade antenna.

Photo: Peter Anthoni

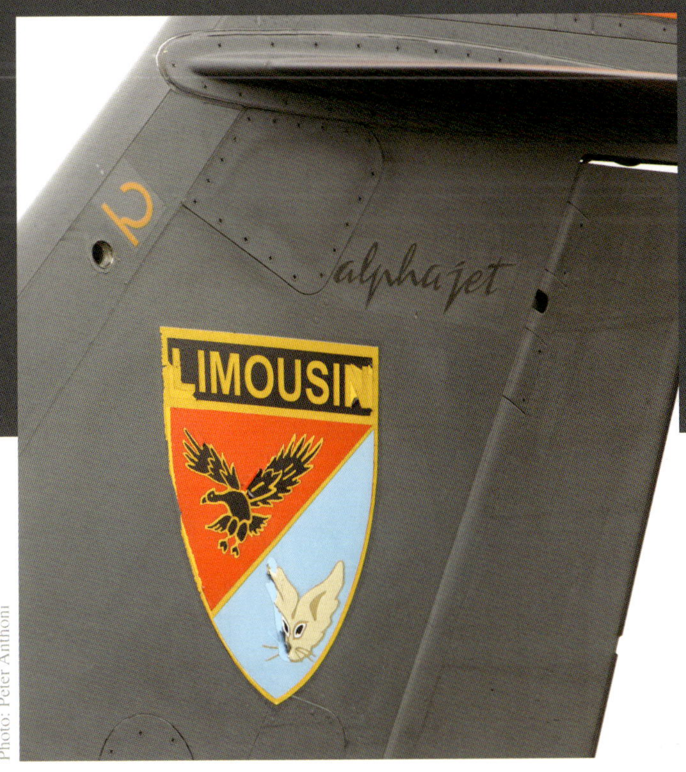

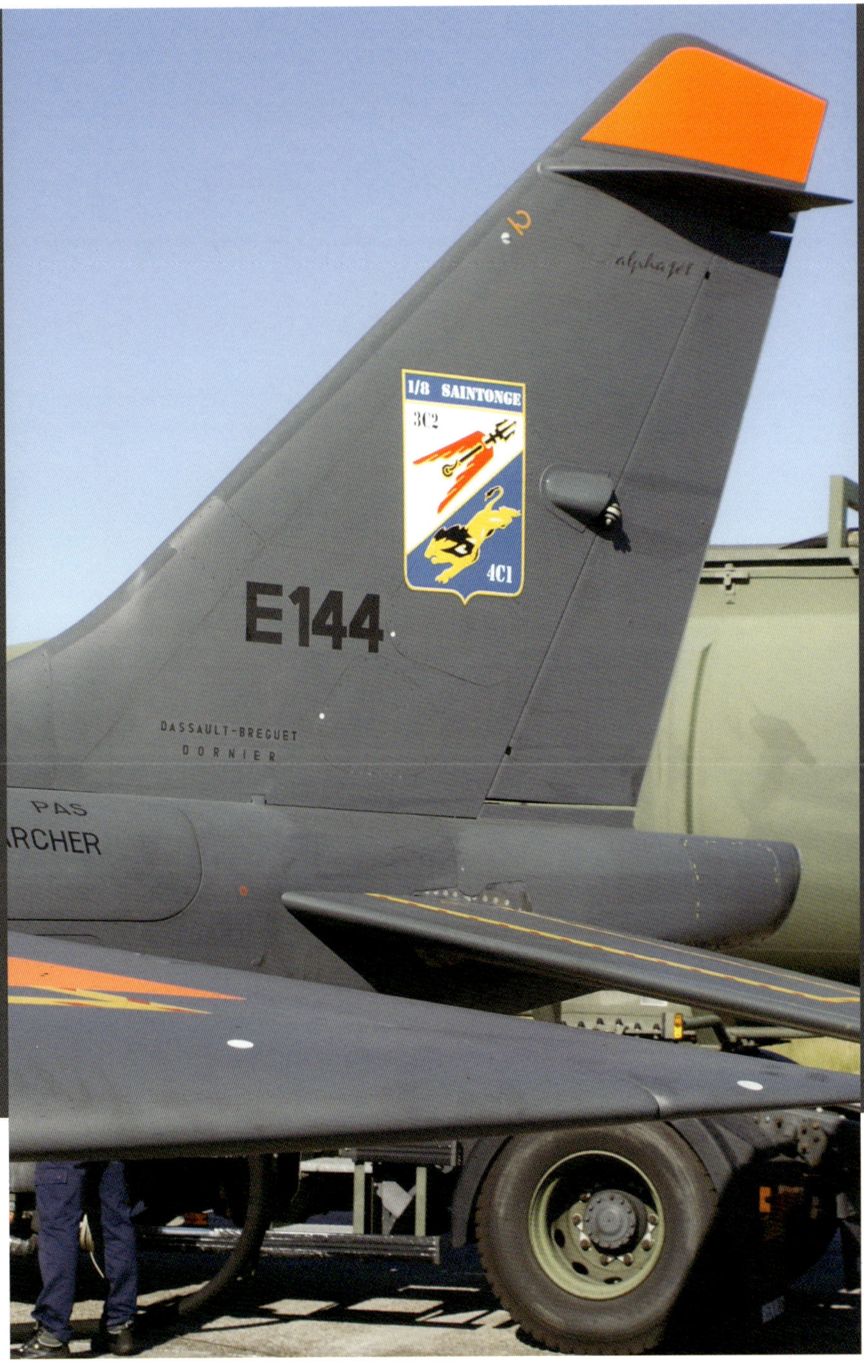

Photo: Robert Pied

Above: Look at the proximity of the speed brake to the vertical tail. The base of the tail - or rather the far end of the fuselage - houses the tail light.

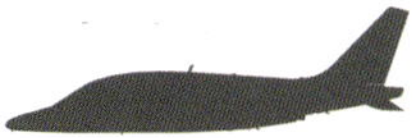

Patrouille de France

The most famous Alpha Jets are those of the French demonstration team "Patrouille de France". The team can retrace its history back to 1931, which makes it the oldest demo team in the world. It has been flying the Alpha Jet since 1981 and has been performing all over the world. Before transfering to the Alpha Jet, the team flew some legendary aircraft, such as the F-84G Thunderjet, Ouragan, Mystère IV and Fouga Magister. The team comprises of 10 jets - 8 that perform the show and 2 spares - and has a ground crew of 35 mechanics. For some occasions, the team performs fly-bys with 9 aircraft in diamond formation, like on Bastille Day. The unit is based at Base Aérienne 701 Salon-de-Provence in Bouches-du-Rhône, in the south of France. I guess there are worse places to be stationned!

Each year, the team builds up a new show that has to be validated by the Chief of Staff of the Armée de l'Air. I can't imagine there's any stress involved when performing the new display for the first time in front of the boss - ahum...

The Patrouille de France has been thrilling spectators all over the world for 30 years, flying with the Alpha Jet. On the centerline of the aircraft, a smoke pod is installed, enabling the jets to trail the famous red-white-and-blue of France's flag. Notice in the photo below that the aircraft is equipped with the old-style Mk.4 ejection seat.

Below: A neat line-up of Alpha Jets of the Patrouille de France. During the 2017 air show season, the Patrouille de France did a tour in the US and received a special tail marking, showing an artistic rendering of the stars and bars.

Photo: Jens Schymura

Photo: Kris Christiaens

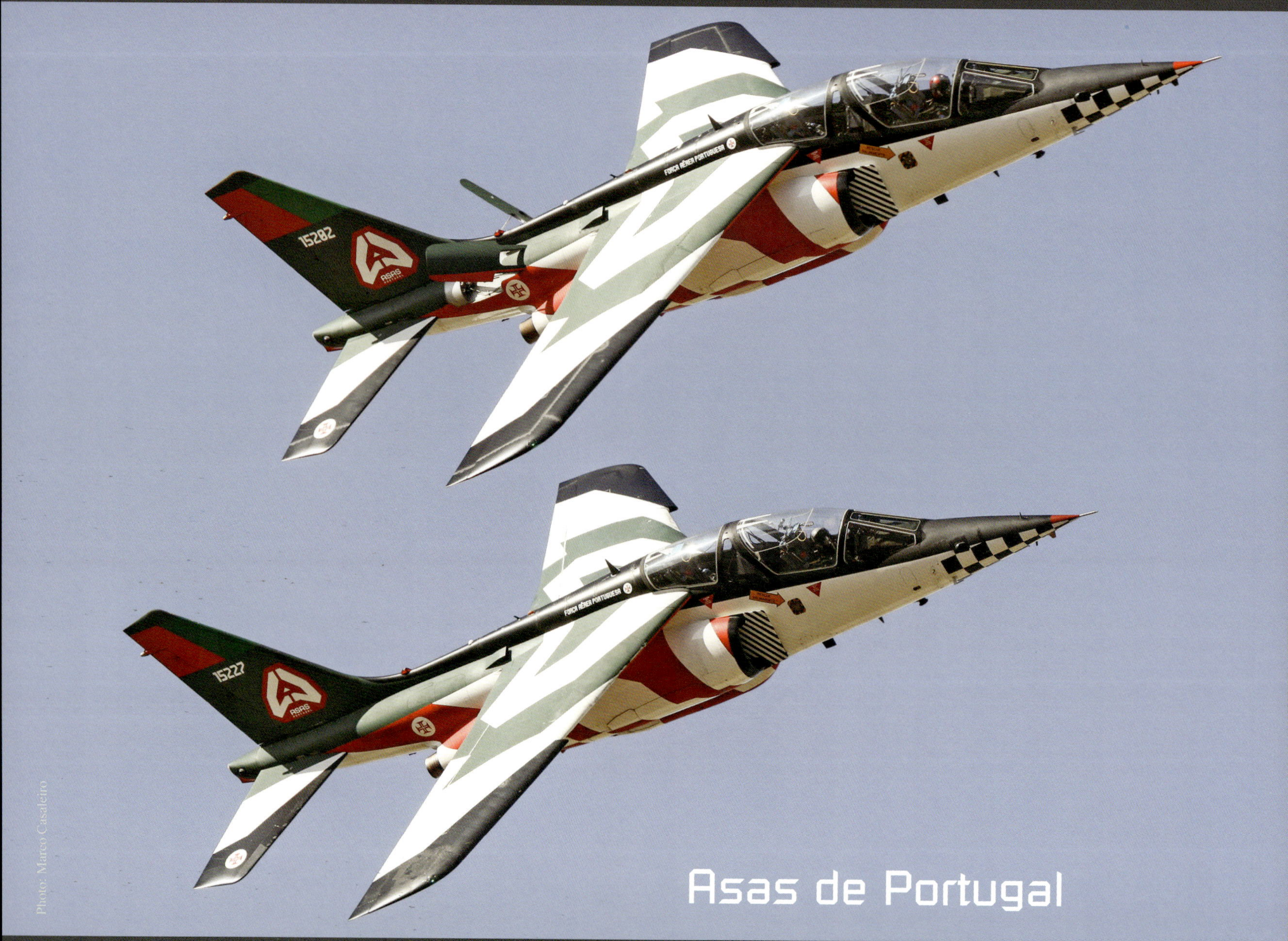

Asas de Portugal

Until 2010, the Portuguese Air Force had a demonstration team called the Asas de Portugal - The Wings of Portugal - which consisted of a pair of Alpha Jets, flying in very tight formations. The history of the team goes back to 1977, when it was formed and operated the Cessna T-37C. For 13 years, the aircraft, sporting the national colours, flew with 6 aircraft at airshows around Europe.

In the final season of 1990, one of the T-37s crashed during a training session when one of the wings suffered a structural failure. Following the crash, which unfortunately killed the pilot, all T-37s were grounded and inspected. All but 5 in the fleet had small cracks in the wings and the type was withdrawn from service. Seven years later, the team was re-activated, flying the Alpha Jet.

Above: One of the Asas de Portugal jets banks in the summer sun, ready for another display. Portugal's Alpha Jets are former Luftwaffe aircraft that were purchased back in 1993 when a replacement was sought for the Fiat G-91 and T-38 Talon. The Alpha Jet A proved to be a perfect match and 50 were acquired, of which 5 were a source for spare parts.

Right: The Asas de Portugal were welcome visitors to many airshows around Europe. For long transfers, the aircraft were equipped with external fuel tanks - pylons and tanks were painted black to match the aircraft's livery. Notice the opened-up speedbrake in the background.

On to the aft fuselage of the Alpha Jet. On top of the engine nacelles, an air intake is installed that provides the engines with cooling air. Below it is a smaller air exhaust. The photo to the right shows the intake on the port side in close-up.

Left & above: The starboard side with the air exhaust on the engine bay door. Look at the quick-release buttons of the latter. The photo to the left shows the exhaust overflow of the fuel tanks.

Photo: Marco Casaleiro

Above: A Portuguese Alpha Jet A is landing at Beja and has it's speed brakes deployed.

Right: The tail light in detail.

Far right: Looking up at the tail boom with the horizontal tails. Look at the raised rivets on the trailing edge of the stabilisors.

Photo: Robert Pied

Photo: Robert Pied

Left: The aft fuselage avionics bay on the port side of the aircraft. In the maintenance section of the book, we'll have a look inside.
Below: The aft fuselage with the base of the horizontal tails.

Photo: Duke Archives

Photo: Robert Pied

Below: The air intake on the aft fuselage on the starboard side.
Right: The engine exhaust of the SNECMA Turbomeca Larzac 04-C5 turbofan engine. Look at the coloration in different shades of bronze.

Photo: Duke Archives

Photo: Robert Pied

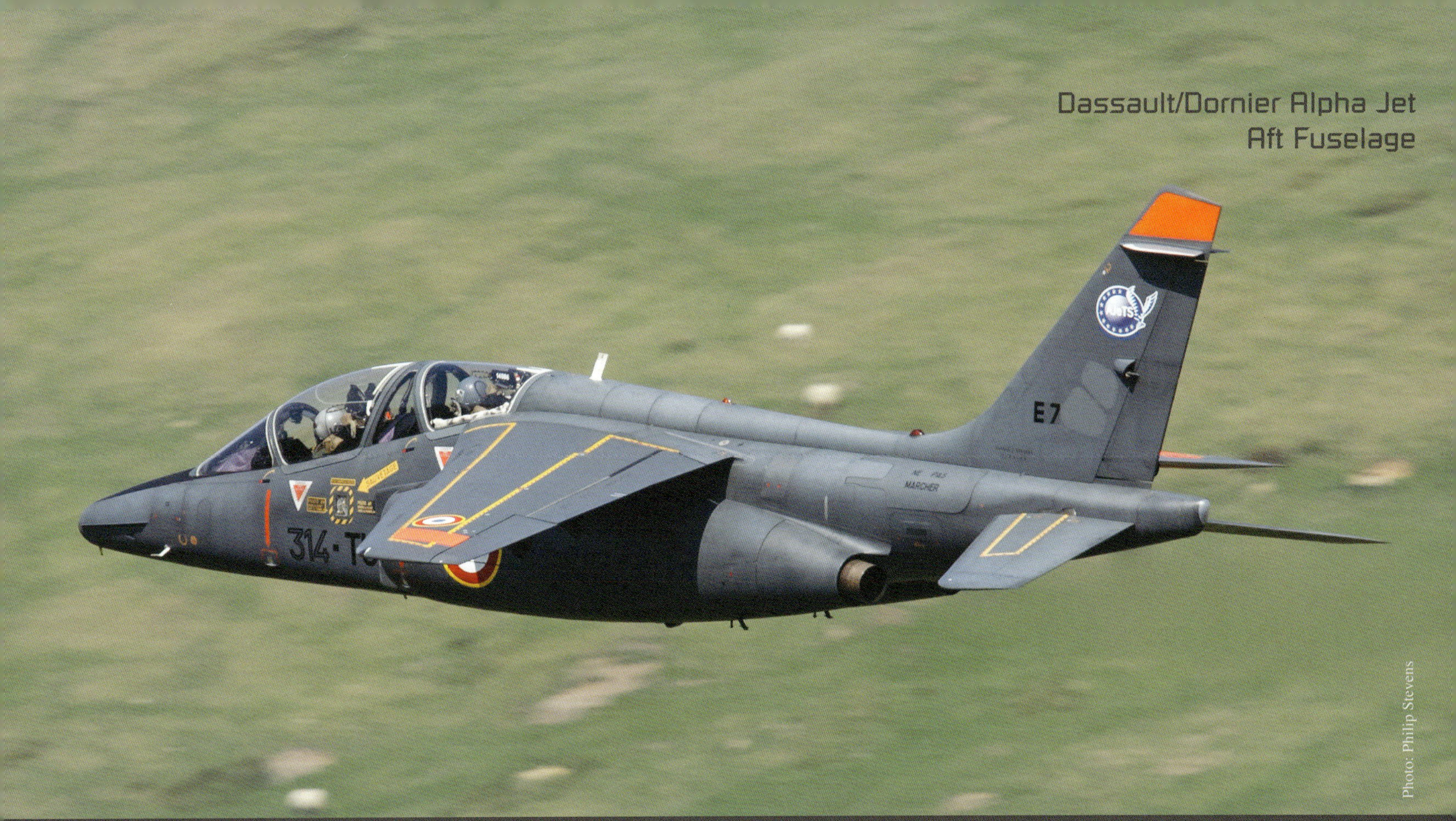

Photo: Philip Stevens

Photo: Robert Pied

Above: A French Alpha Jet of AJets is passing low through the Mach Loop in Wales. Notice the different shades of the panels on the spine and vertical tale and the Martin-Baker Mk.4 seats.

Photo: Robert Pied

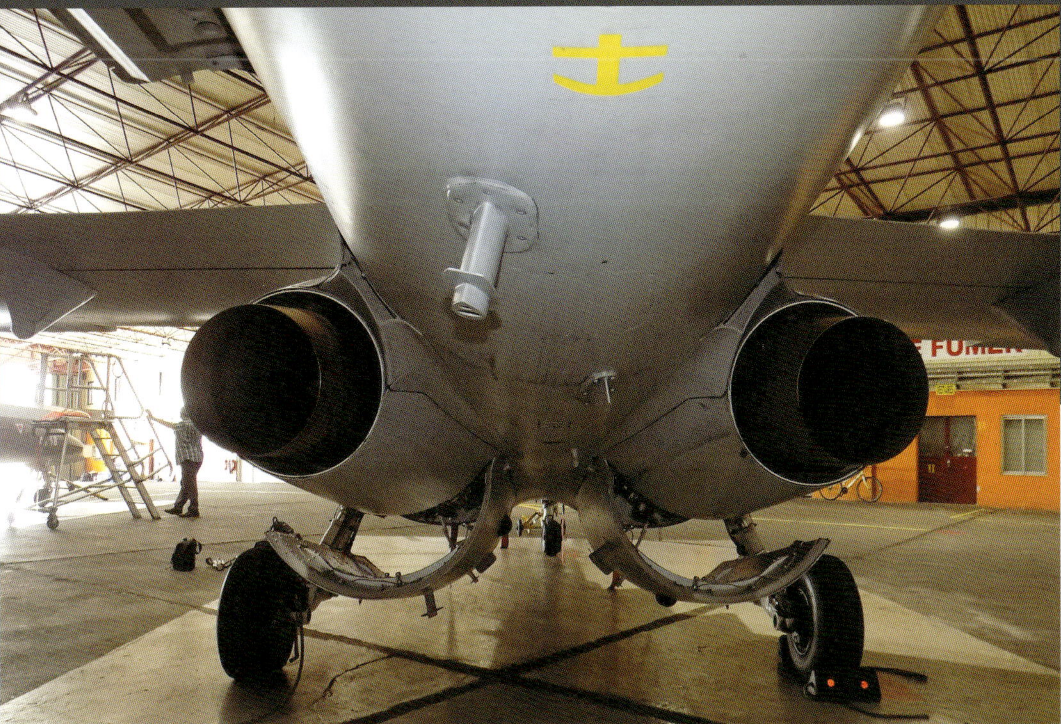

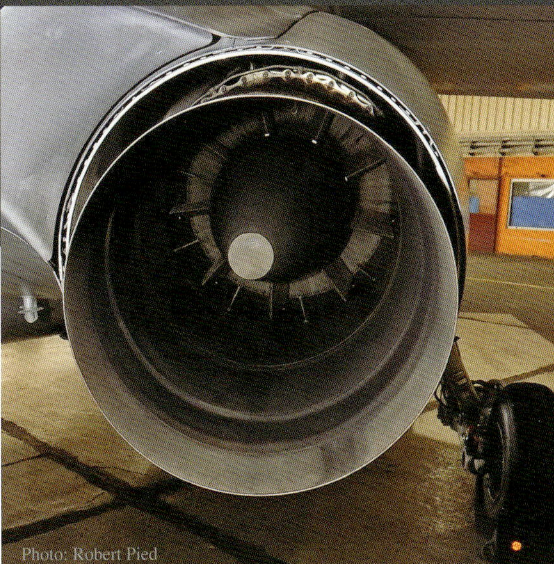

Above: The same aircraft as the big photo on the opposite page, seen from the starboard side. Looks like an old F-104 boarding ladder still comes in handy!

Left: In the front of the aircraft, on the port side, the LOX - Liquid Oxygen container can be found. Notice the structure of the door, which opens by means of two simple push-buttons.

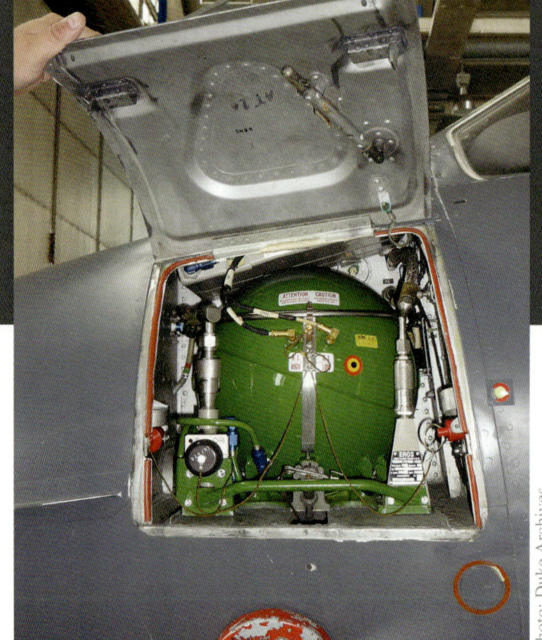

Photo: Kris Christiaens

Maintaining the Alpha Jet

Like with every aircraft, the Alpha Jet only flies as good as it does because of the team of mechanics and engineers that keep it in perfect condition. In this chapter, we bring you a closer look at the Alpha Jet in the different stages of maintenance. Look at the many details in the photo above: AT-21 has been placed on jacks and had its wings removed - they are placed on a metalic shelf behind it - as well as its canopies, ejection seats and even horizontal tails.

Left: Before the Belgian aircraft could be shipped to Canada's Top Aces, they were checked and the engines were removed and crated. Fortunately for us, this was the perfect opportunity to do some maintenance photographs!
This photo shows two Alpha Jets in the maintenance hangar at Beauvechain Air Base in Belgium - the one closest to the camera has a cradle placed on top of the fuselage, which is used to install or remove the engines. The starboard one is already sitting on a special dolly.

Below: The compartment on the port side of the nose, where the liquid oxygen container is placed. A full container allows for ten hours of flying.

Photo: Guillaume Friart

Photo: Robert Pied

On the port side of the fuselage, aft of the engine exhaust, an avionics bay is located. These photos show the interior of the bay from all sides, with the top left one the interior of the door. This bay contains the Electric Power Converter and the Gyroscope. Like the front bay, this bay is opened by means of two quick release buttons.

Photo: Robert Pied

Photo: Duke Archives

Left & below: On the starboard side of the fuselage, another avionics bay is located. Extensive maintenance is done in different cycles, usually every 30 or 36 months or after 700 to 1,000 flying hours on the airframe. During these overhauls, the entire structure of the aircraft, both internally and externally is checked. All flight control systems, hinges, engines, hydraulics and fuel systems have to be checked.

Photo: Robert Pied

Photo: Robert Pied

Left: This photo shows the pressure refuelling point on the starboard side of the aircraft, located between the air intake and the main landing gear. Notice how the door slides down when opened. The Alpha Jet can also be fuelled by means of a gravity refuelling point located on top of the aircraft, on the port side, just aft of the wing base. The Alpha Jet has a maximum fuel capacity of 1,520 kg.

Photo: Robert Pied

Above: This close-up of the starboard side avionics bay shows the internal structure and the bay door. Notice the equipment and wires running in the bay.

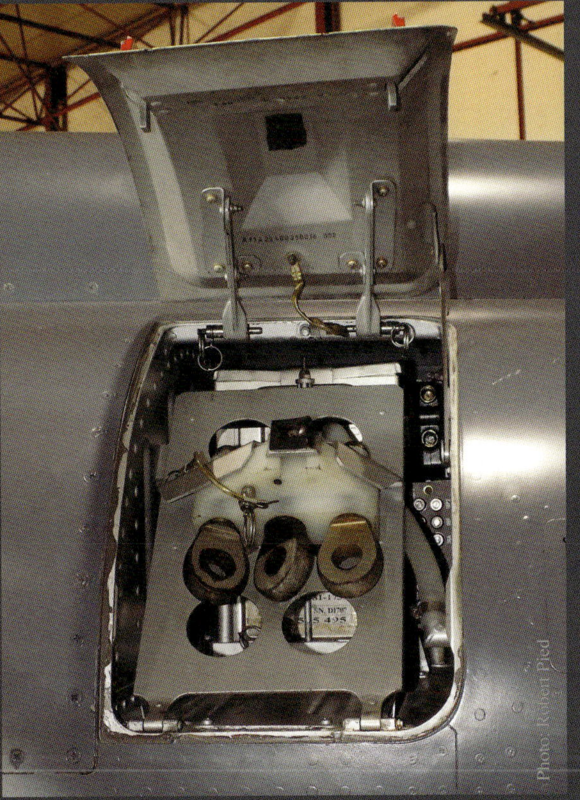

Far left: On the port side of the fuselage, immediately in front of the main landing gear bay, the armament panel is located.

Left: Also on the port side of the fuselage, behind the wings and in front of the avionics bay, a small bay door gives access to the battery compartment.

Below: Sitting on a custom made dolly, these are the gun pods for the DEFA 30 mm gun which can be carried on the centreline of the aircraft. They carry up to 150 rounds. Alpha Jet As are capable of being loaded with a 27 mm Mauser BK-27 gun.

Above: This Alpha Jet has seen some extensive maintenance; the nose cone has been removed and all the glass of the windscreen is taken out of the frames. Look at the fully extended nose wheel. On the starboard side, some panels have been removed to check the equipment and internal structure. Notice that the wings have been removed as well.

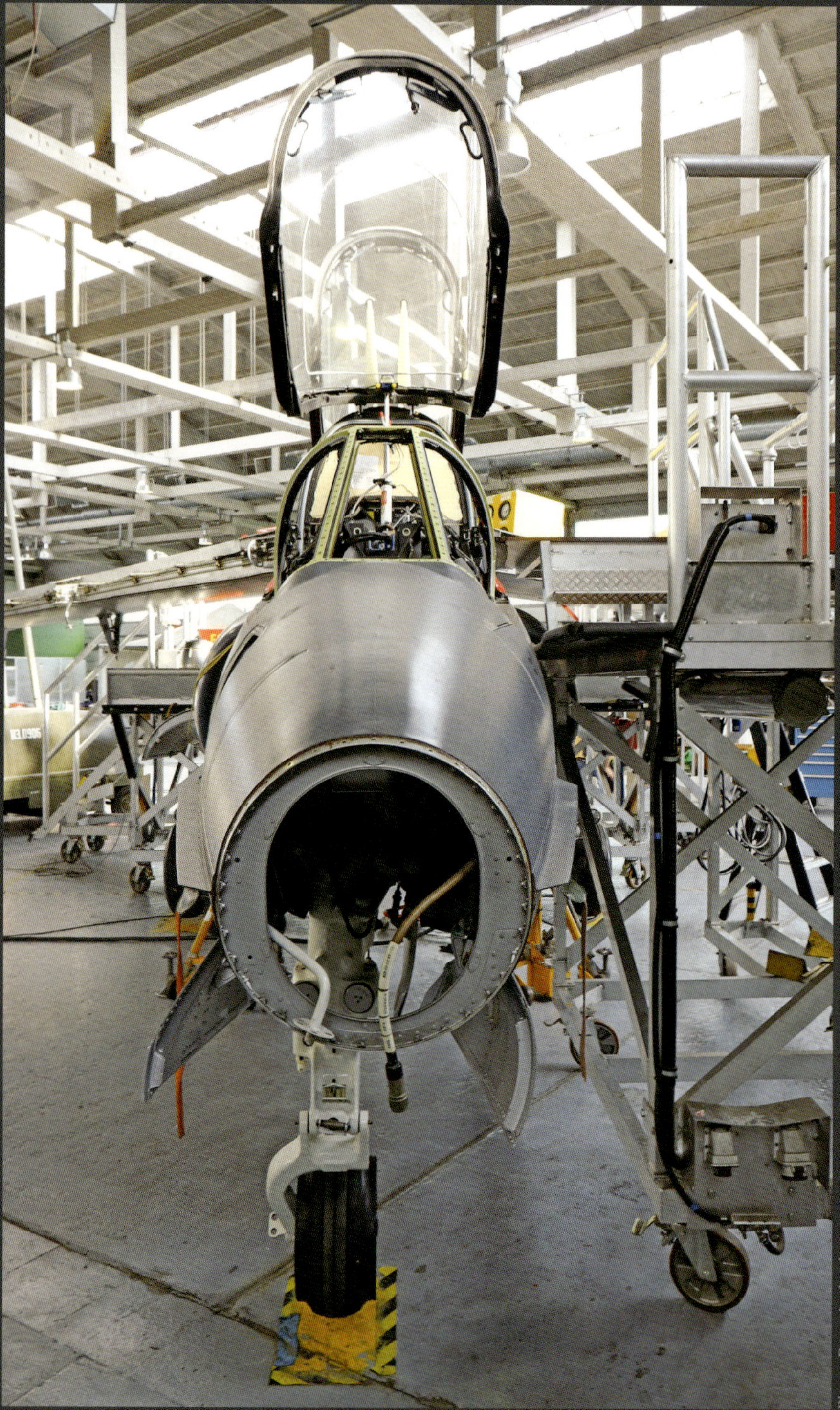

Left: The structure of the windscreen in detail with the glass removed. Notice the structure of the area between the two cockpits, clearly visible now that the ejections seats have been taken out. Look at the canopy actuator.

Below: This is quite an interesting view of the aft part of the pilots instrument panel with the covers removed. Notice the cables running from the instruments.

Photo: Peter Anthoni

Photo: Peter Anthoni

Left: A close-up of the area behind the front ejection seat. Notice the air conditionning vent on the starboard side of the cockpit.

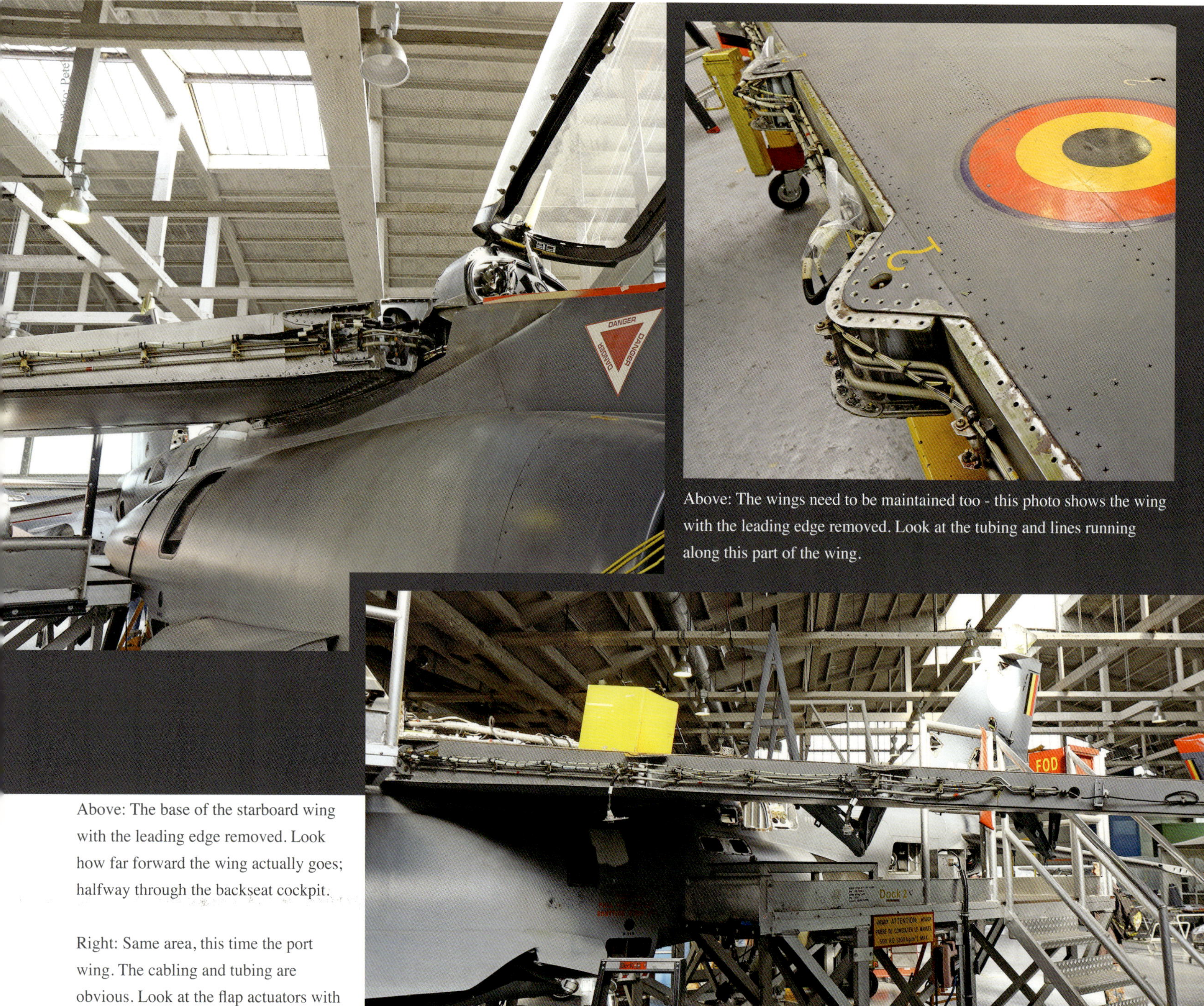

Above: The wings need to be maintained too - this photo shows the wing with the leading edge removed. Look at the tubing and lines running along this part of the wing.

Above: The base of the starboard wing with the leading edge removed. Look how far forward the wing actually goes; halfway through the backseat cockpit.

Right: Same area, this time the port wing. The cabling and tubing are obvious. Look at the flap actuators with the covers removed.

Photo: Peter Anthoni

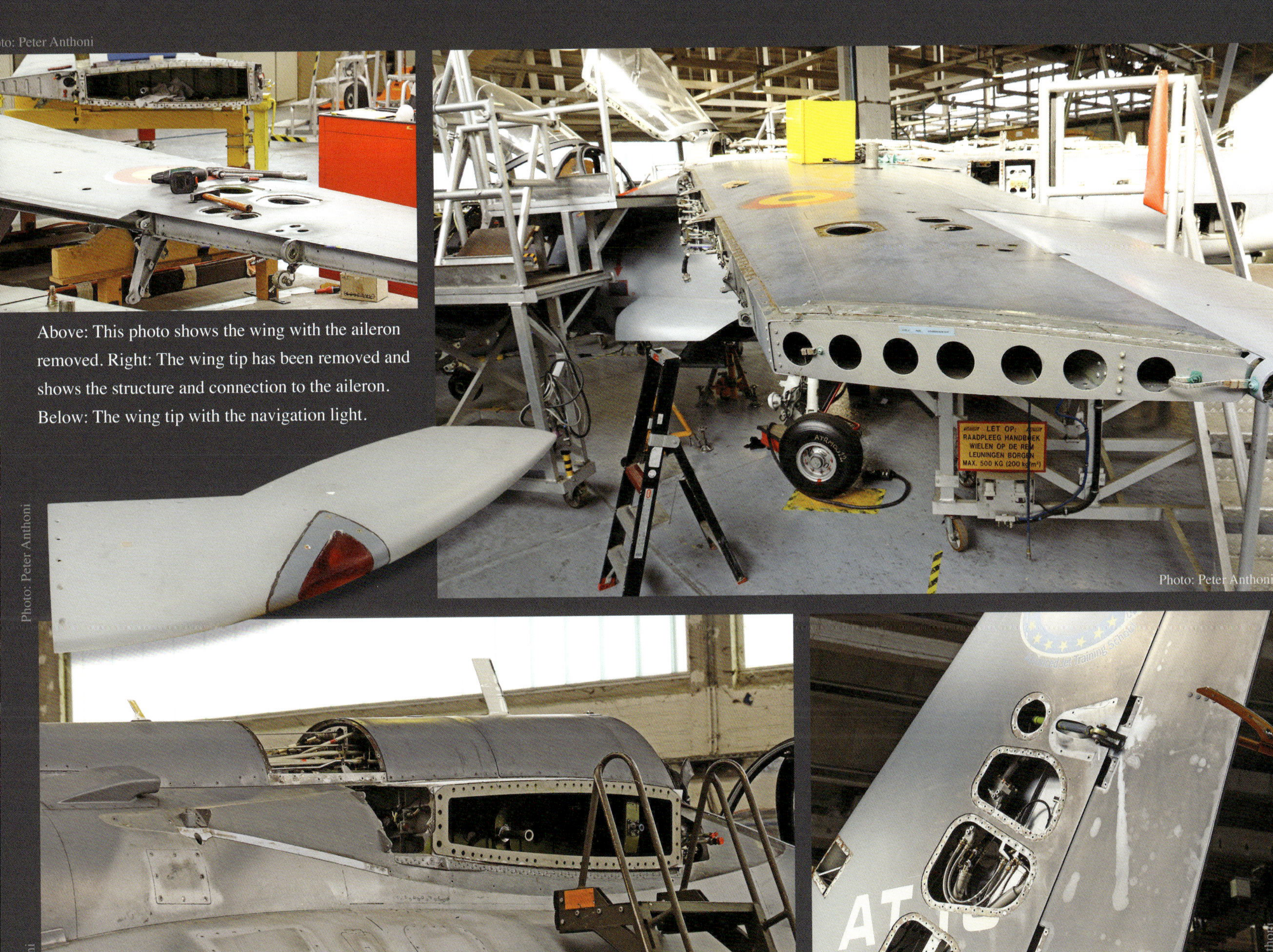

Above: This photo shows the wing with the aileron removed. Right: The wing tip has been removed and shows the structure and connection to the aileron. Below: The wing tip with the navigation light.

Above: The wing of this Alpha Jet has been removed as well as one of the spine panels, showing the cables and tubing underneath it. When bolted down panels are removed and replaced, a quick layer of paint is sprayed on the screws, with this weathering patern as a result.

Above: The vertical tail with some of the inspection panels removed as wel as the tail cone. Notice the rudder actuator with the cover removed.

Photo:Kris Christiaens

Photo: Duke Archives

Photo: Duke Archives

Above: The empty battery compartment on the aft part of the fuselage. The top photo shows a great scene in the maintenance hangar. The engines have been removed and the canopies are placed on a special cart. Look at the inside structure of the wings to the right. And it looks like the speed brake has been checked and stripped of its paint.

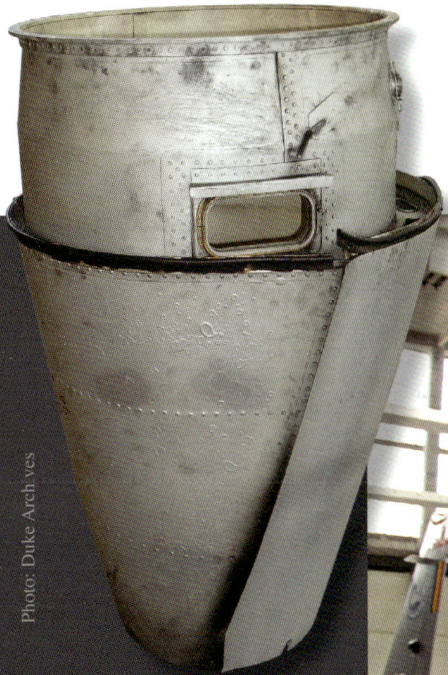

Photo: Duke Archives

Above: The tail section of the engine cover.
Below: These photos show the port and starboard engine bay with the engine removed. Look at the colour and the tubing that is fixed to the firewalls. The engine, the SNECMA Turbomeca Larzac 04-C5, is very compact with a length of just 1,18 meter.

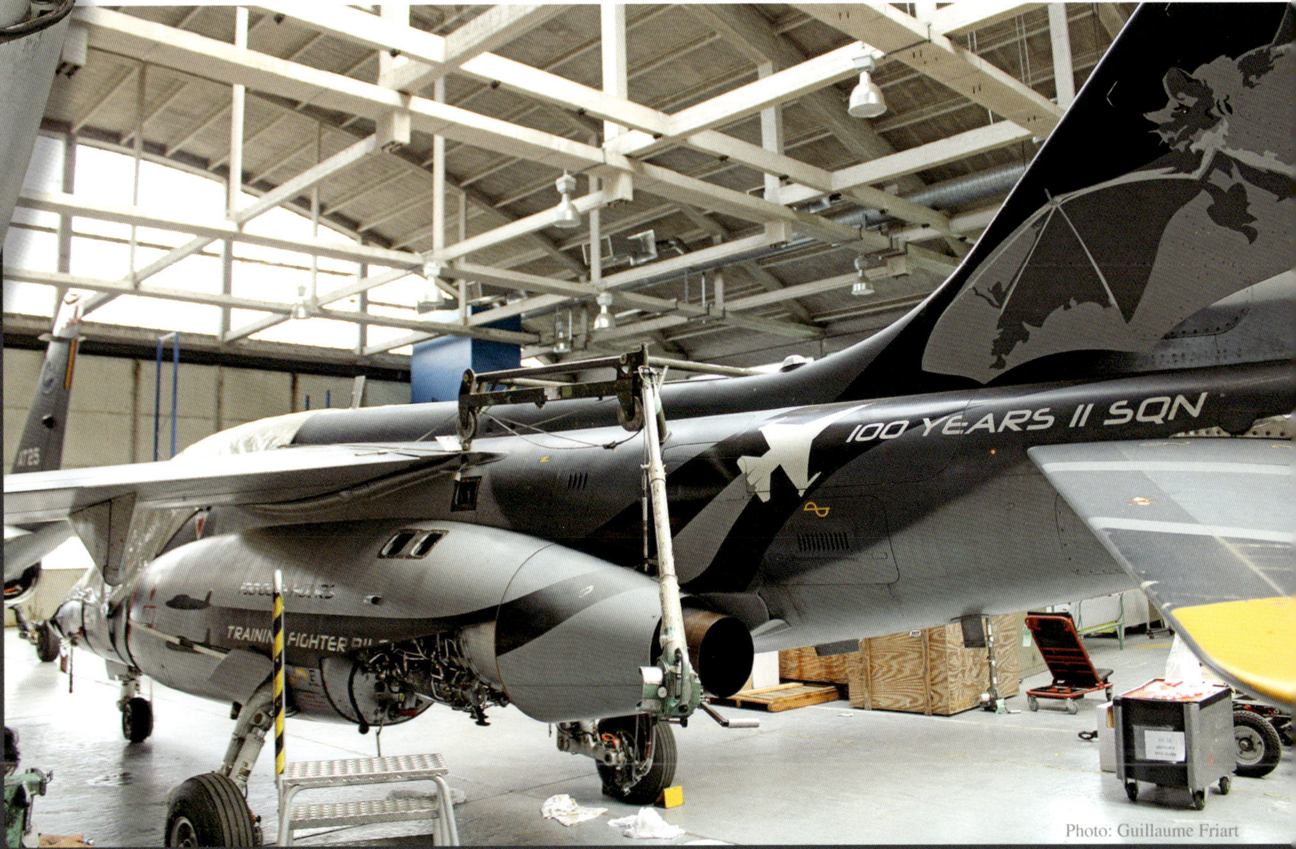

Photo: Guillaume Friart

Photo: Duke Archives

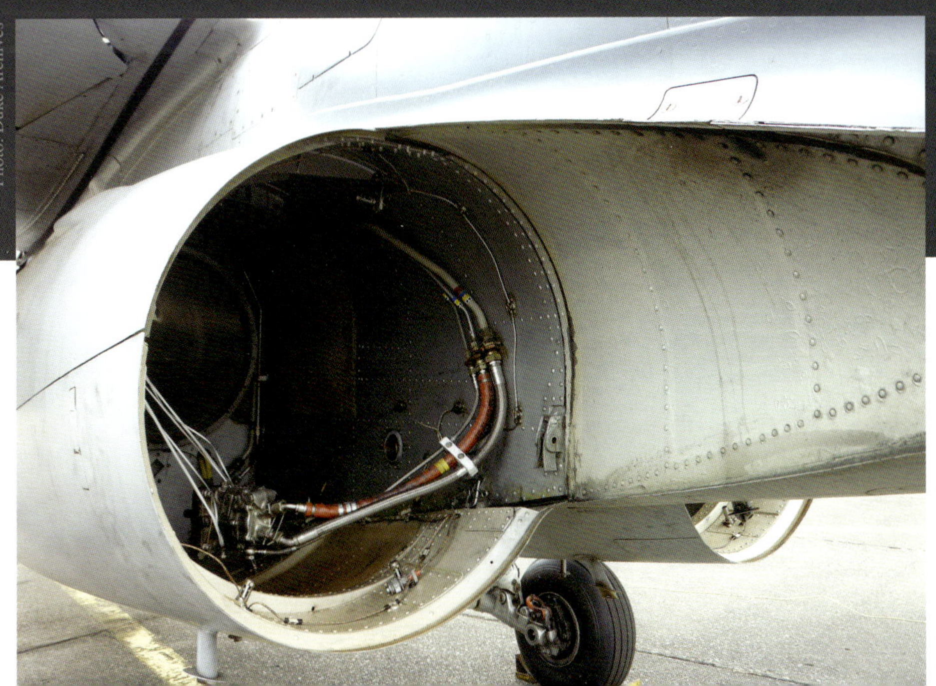

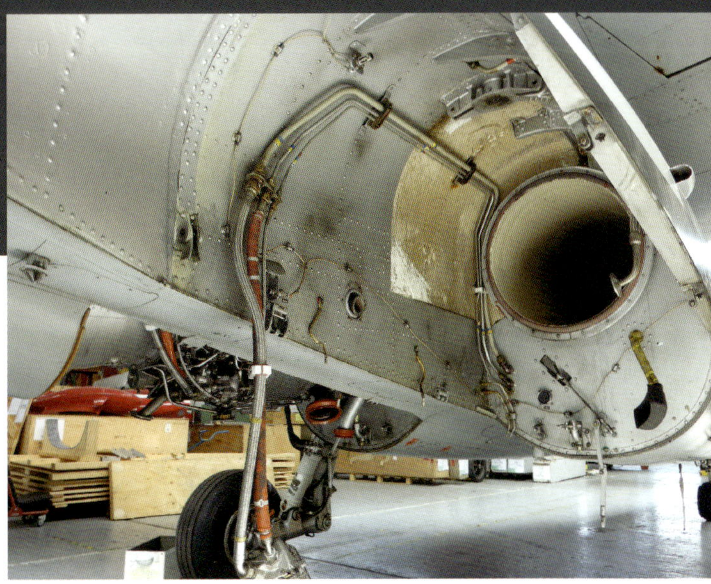

Photo: Duke Archives

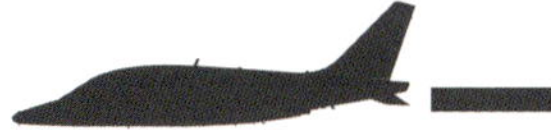

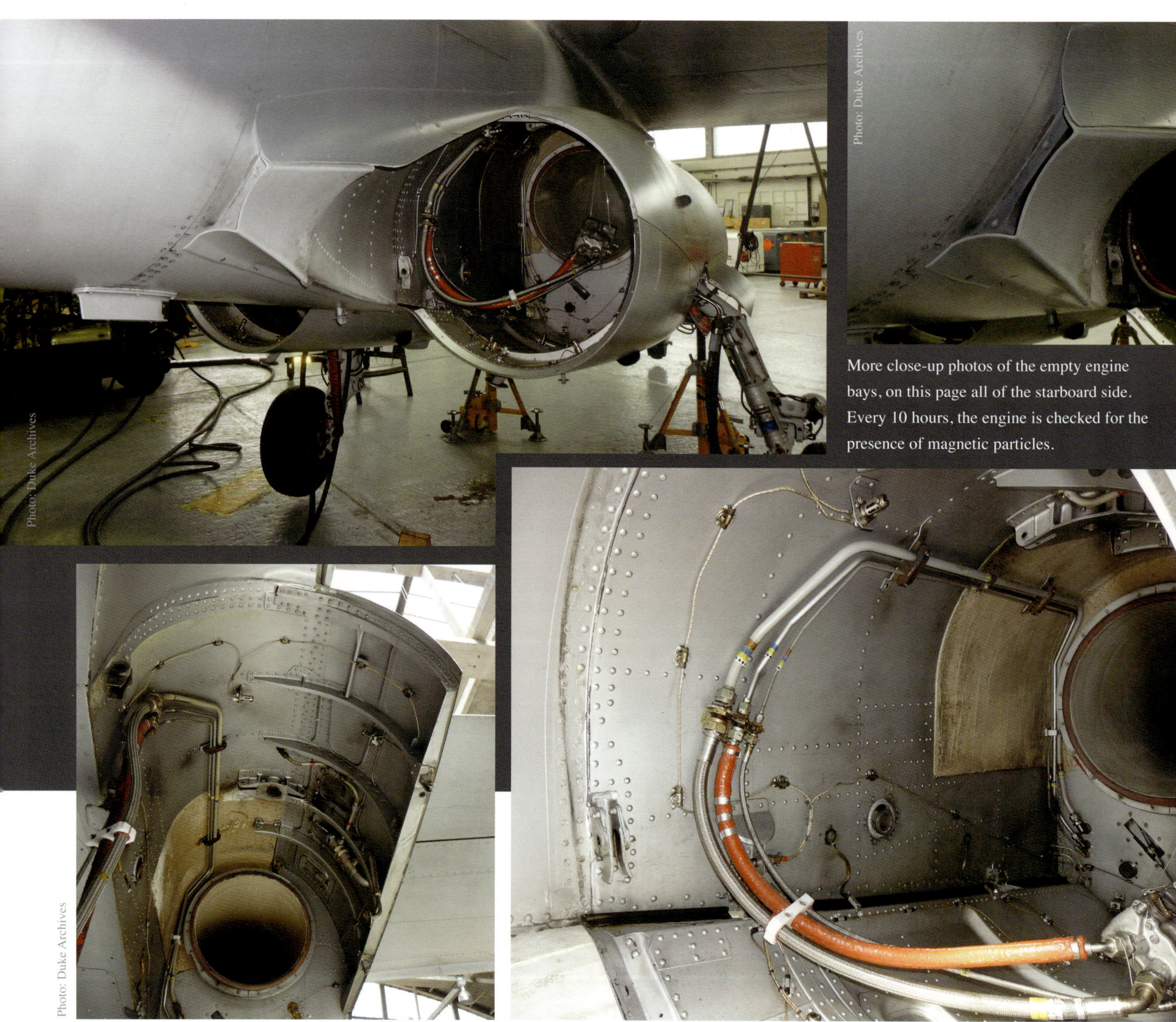

More close-up photos of the empty engine bays, on this page all of the starboard side. Every 10 hours, the engine is checked for the presence of magnetic particles.

Photo: Duke Archives

Photo: Duke Archives

Photo: Duke Archives

Photo: Duke Arch

Right: This photo shows the port engine bay with the large access door below installed - compare with the photos on page 91, where these doors are removed.

The engines are checked at frequent intervals, but every 600 hours, they are removed from the aircraft and completely checked and where necessary, parts are replaced. During the engine maintenance, endoscopic and vibration tests are performed. When maintenance has been done, the engine is tested before it goes back into the aircraft. Notice in these photos the details of the forward wall, with the air intake duct and the area behind which the main gear bay is located.

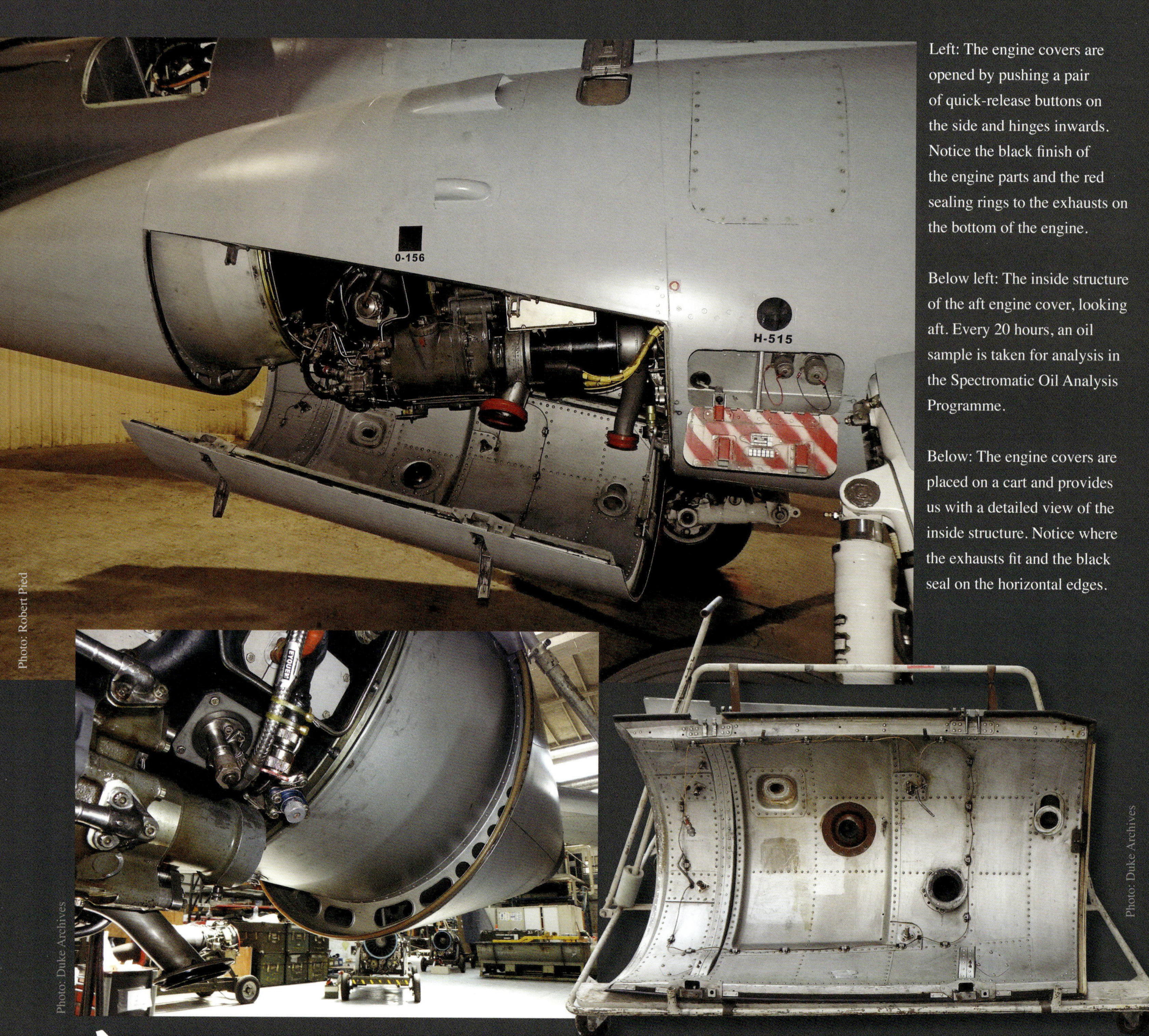

Left: The engine covers are opened by pushing a pair of quick-release buttons on the side and hinges inwards. Notice the black finish of the engine parts and the red sealing rings to the exhausts on the bottom of the engine.

Below left: The inside structure of the aft engine cover, looking aft. Every 20 hours, an oil sample is taken for analysis in the Spectromatic Oil Analysis Programme.

Below: The engine covers are placed on a cart and provides us with a detailed view of the inside structure. Notice where the exhausts fit and the black seal on the horizontal edges.

Photo: Robert Pied

Photo: Duke Archives

Photo: Duke Archives

Above: The engine bay door hinges inwards and can be fixed in place by means of a support brace to the front of the door. Notice the air exhaust above the engine bay.

Right: The engine exhausts nozzles of the SNECMA Turbomeca Larzac 04-C5 are slightly canted outwards.

Compared to fighter jets such as the F-16 or Rafale, the ratio flight hours to maintenance hours is quite low; it takes 7 hours of maintenance for every hour of flying.

Photo: Duke Archives

Time to take a closer look at the SNECMA Turbomeca Larzac 04-C5 of the Alpha Jet, which is an axial flow, twin-spool, bypass turbofan engine. The engine is extremely compact, comes in at a length of 1,18 meter and has a dry weight of just 295 kg. The photos above show the aft part of the engine from the side and up-front. It is built up with a compressor in two low pressure stages and four high pressure stages. The Turbine Inlet temperature is 1,130 degrees.

Right: The engine and the aft engine cover with the exhaust fixed to it.

Right: This photo shows just how compact the engine really is, with the aft part of the engine to the left in the photo.

Below: The forward part of the engine with the compressor blades. Look at the light blue colour on the inside of the inlet, which is 45,2 cm in diameter. The cut-out photo to the right of it shows the entire engine, with the aft cover fixed to it, on a dolly. Look at the details of the fuelpipes and connections running all over it.
An interesting anecdote on the engine is that when it was in development, it was first tested on a Lockheed Constellation. Now there's a cool combination!

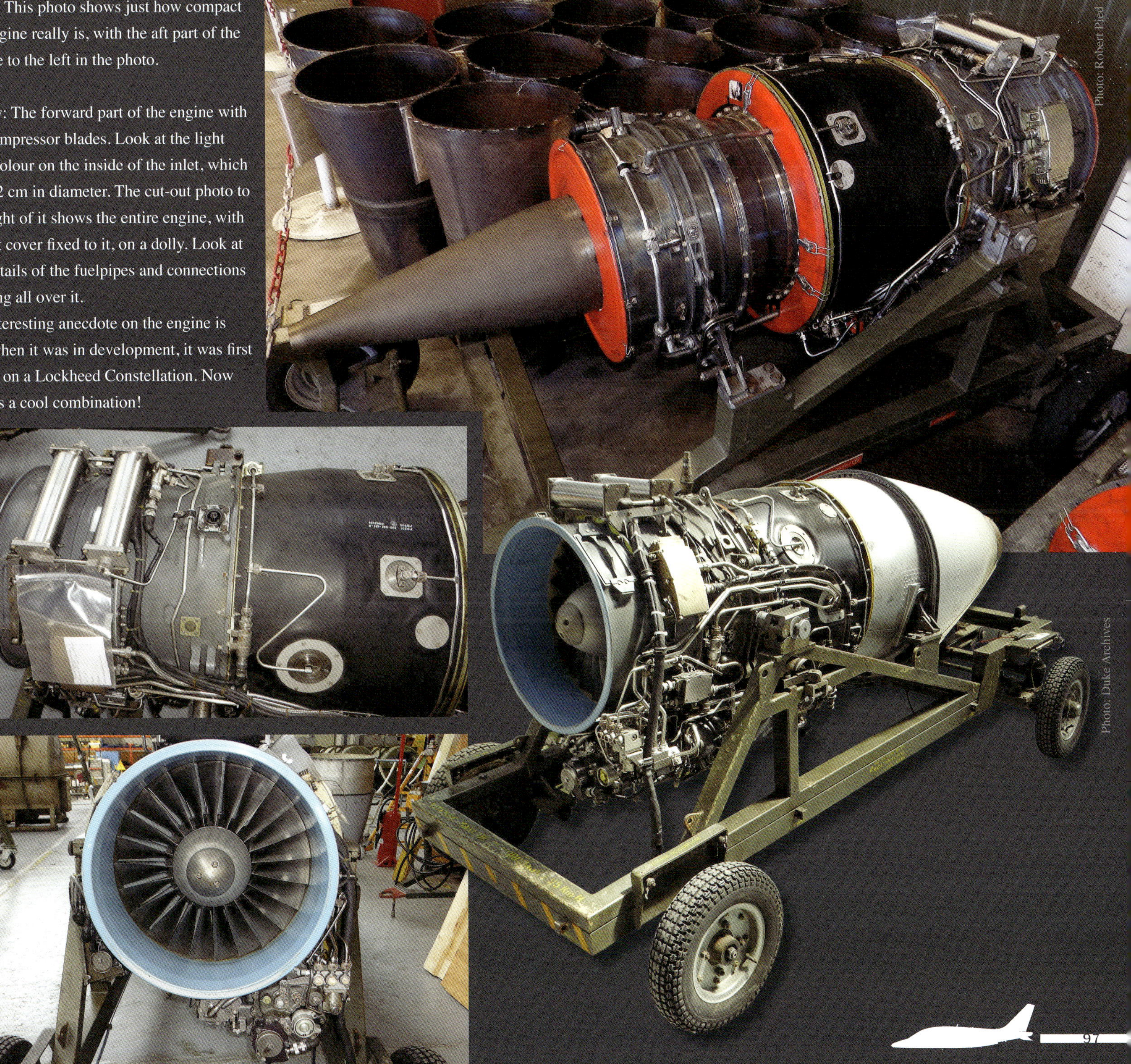

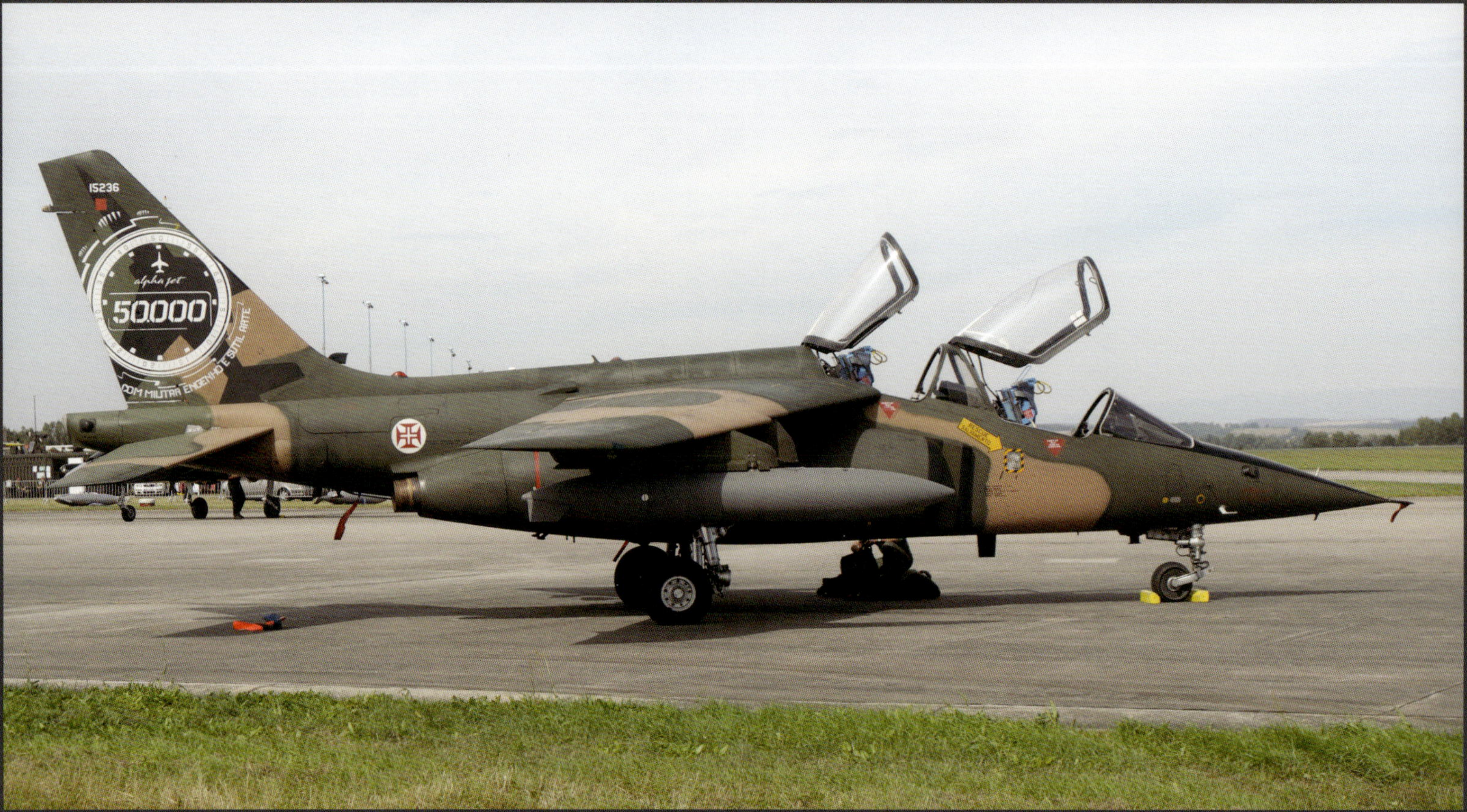

The Alpha Jet can be loaded with 2 pylons under each wing, as can be seen in the photo above of a Portuguese Alpha Jet A. Notice the different profiles of the pylons. The photos left and below show the outboard pylon in detail, while the one on the opposite page is of the inboard pylon, just inwards of the dog tooth on the leading edge.

Right: This Belgian Air Force Alpha Jet has the inboard pylons installed, ready for an air-to-ground excercise using the practice bombs loaded on the SUU-20A. The pylons are fixed and can't be jettisoned in flight. The Alpha Jet has a fifth station on the centreline which in this case is loaded with a gun pod containing a DEFA 30 mm gun.

Below right: This close-up is of the gun pod of a German Alpha Jet A, which is equipped with a 27 mm Mauser BK-27 gun.

Photo: Bart Rosselle

Photo: Jens Schymura

Photo: Jens Schymura

Above: The inboard pylon with a rocket pod installed, as carried by a Luftwaffe Alpha Jet A. Notice the difference in profile with those on page 98.

Action !!

Photo: Bart Rosselle

After an avalanche of details, it's always good to show the aircraft in action, both on the ground and in the air. The photo above by Bart Rosselle, shows AT-22 and AT-12 of the Belgian Air Force forming up at the port wing of the aircraft in which he's flying. Notice the gun pack fixed to the belly of AT-12.

The big photo to the right shows AT-33, the last Alpha Jet to be delivered to the Belgian Air Force in July of 1980. Look at the clean lines of this elegant jet! And on this background of a dark blue Atlantic Ocean, the jet's nose looks even more like a dolphin!

Dassault/Dornier Alpha Jet
Action
AT33
Photo: Sirpa

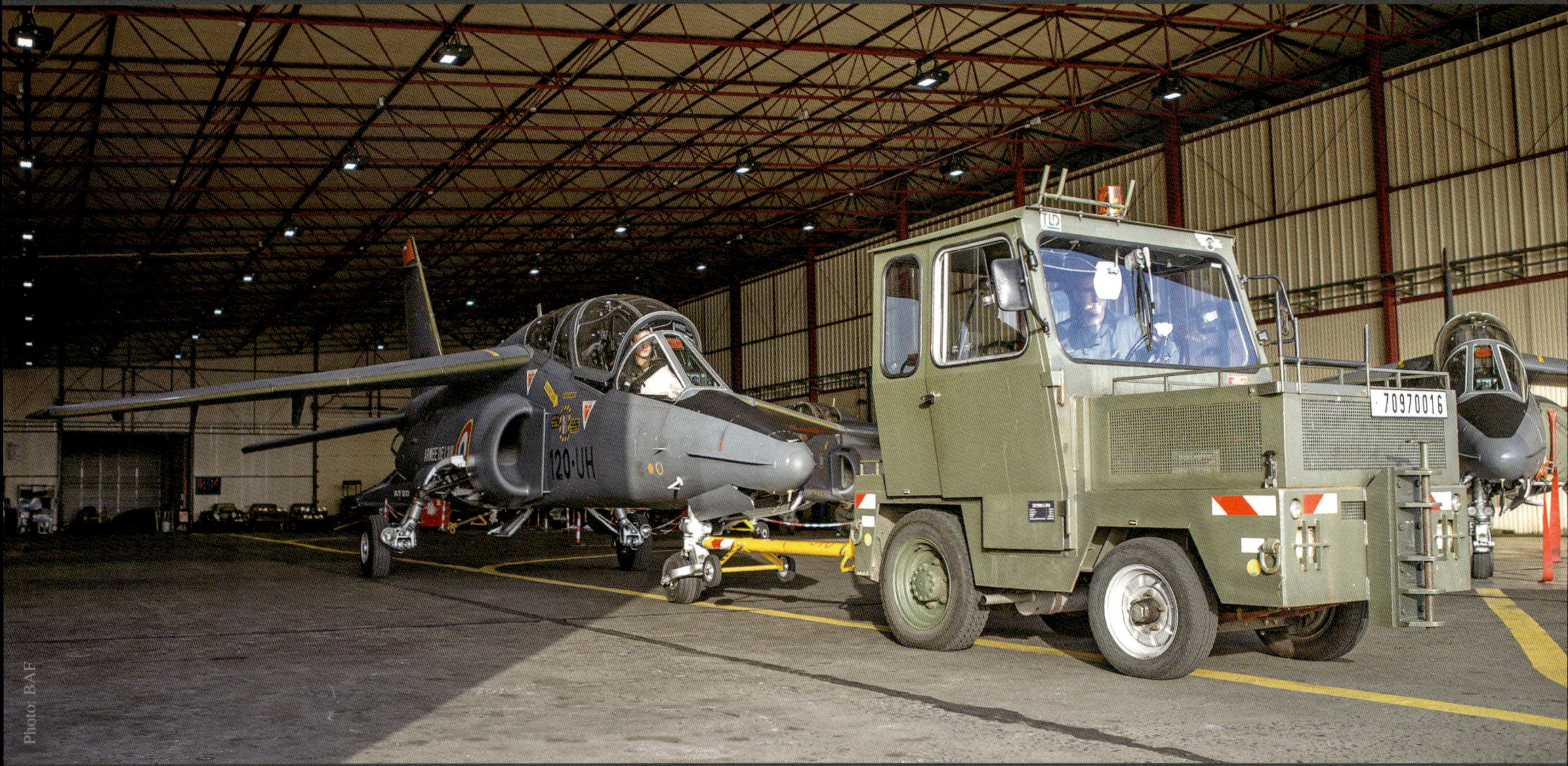

Photo: BAF

Photo: Peter Anthoni

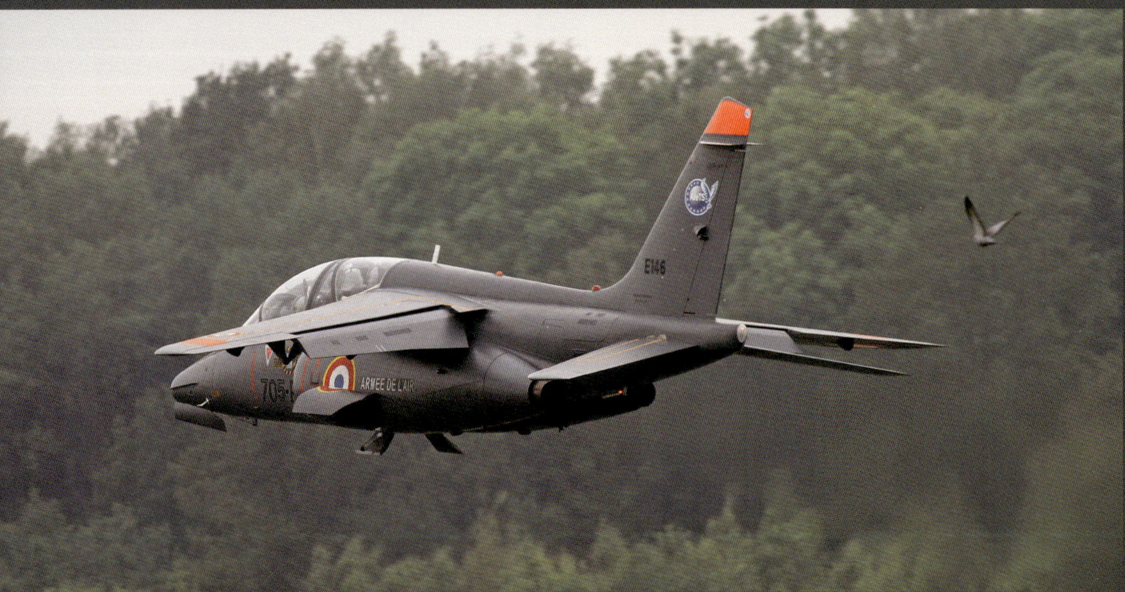

Above: A French Alpha Jet is being pulled out of the hangar at Cazaux Air Base for another day of student-training. Look where the towbar is connected to the nose landing gear.

Left: An Alpha Jet of the Armée de l'Air is taking off and flies in formation with a Mk.1 Pigeon. Look at the landing gear doors, about to be closed and the lowered trailing edge flaps. The Alpha Jet only needs about 400 meter to get airborne. Notice the AJets logo on the vertical tail - Advanced Jet Training School.

Above: 7 Belgian Alpha Jet in a tight formation - now there's a sight! The Alpha Jet is an ideal aircraft for aerobatics and formation flying because of the smooth and stable flying characteristics.

Left: The Alpha Jet has always been a good canvas for the artistic minds of the Belgian Air Force. This aircraft of 7 SQN was painted in this striking livery for the 20th anniversary of the type.

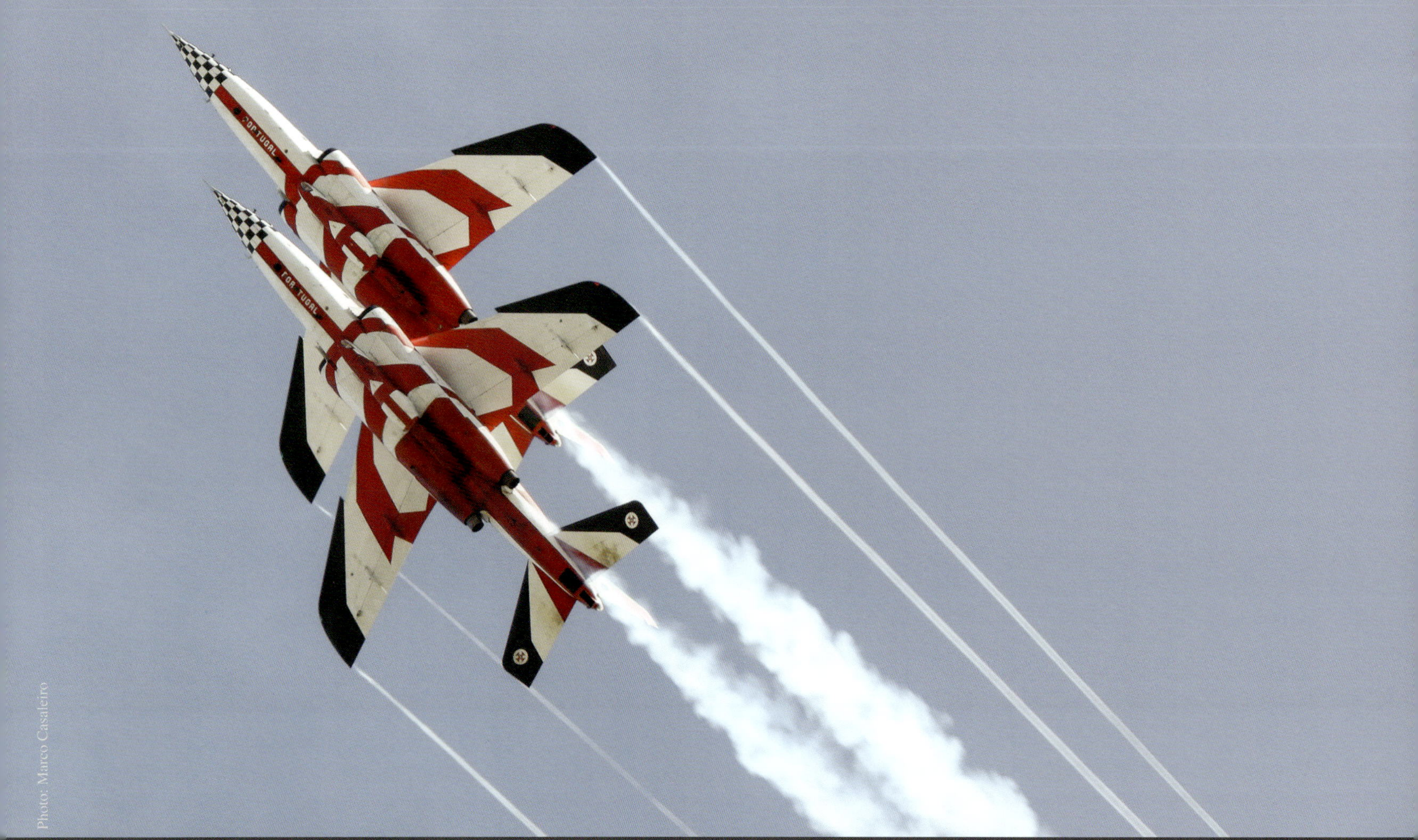

Photo: Marco Casaleiro

Above: Flying in a tight formation and trailing white smoke, the Asas de Portugal are climbing for another spectacular manoeuvre. Notice the team's logo painted on the belly of the aircraft.

Right: This German Alpha Jet A of JaboG 41, based at Husum in North Friesland received a commemorative colour scheme back in 1984, celebrating the 25th anniversary of the Wing. Mockingly called "Hummingbird", the aircraft took part in the flying display during the open day in October 1984. Look at the gun-pod installed underneath the jet.

Photo: Volkhard Waltermann

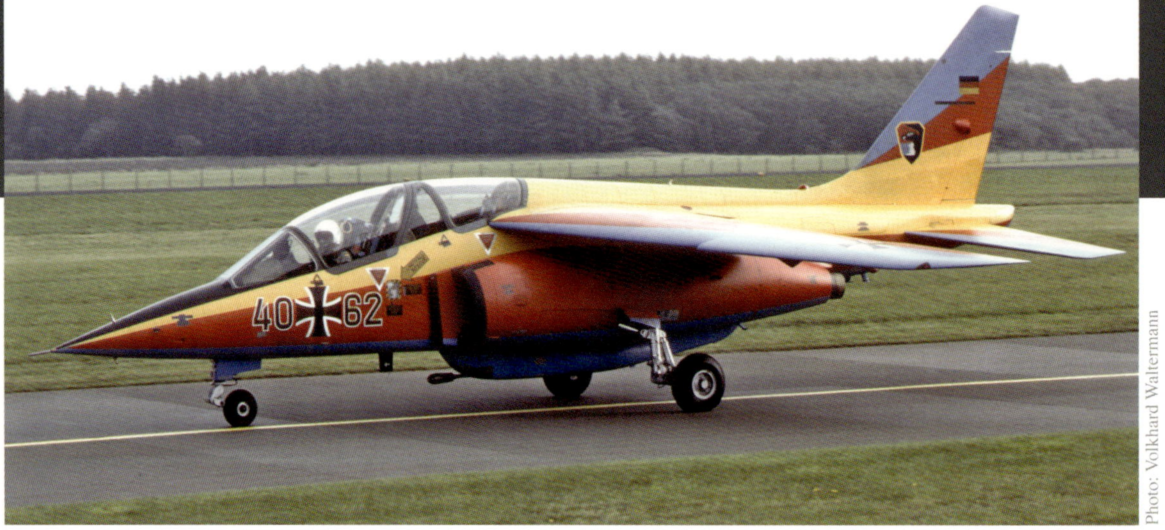

Above: Returning after a formation flight, these Alpha Jets are taxiing back to their parking spots. It being a hot day, the crew have already raised their canopies somewhat. Again, look how wide the main gear is positionned.

Right: This beverage company, which clearly has a big heart for aviation, is another civil operator of a former Luftwaffe Alpha Jet A. I'm never quite sure if I like the way the aircraft are painted, but then again, it's great that they keep flying these aircraft.

Photo: Kris Christiaens

Photo: Kris Christiaens

Alpha Jet Rainmaker

Every now and then you come across a story that is interesting, but you have to check at least twice. Such is the story of a program involving an Alpha Jet of the Royal Moroccan Air Force, called Al Ghait or Rainmaker. One of the effects of climate change is that some countries are confronted with higher temperatures and droughts. Morocco, situated in North Africa on the border of the Sahara desert, has seen a reduction of rainfall in the last two decades by at least 10 per cent, with estimates worsening over the next decades. Because the country's economy relies heavily on agriculture, the government invested in a drought mitigation strategy, which includes new agricultural techniques, conservation measures and ... making it rain. For the latter, one of the country's 24 Alpha Jets was equipped with a Sperry/Honeywell Primus 300SL weather radar which was installed in a modified nose. The flare countermeasures dispenser in the rear fuselage was also modified to launch silver iodide cartridges above clouds, a process called cloud seeding. The process is as follows: the small water drops in the clouds fix themselves onto the silver iodide chrystals, making them heavier, which results in rain. This way, some control can be had on where the rain falls from the clouds. Studies of the Moroccan system has shown an increase in precipitation of around 15 per cent, which can make a big difference in countries hit by drought. It comes at a price though, because the silver iodide is toxic for the environment and for species or humans. As is often the case, both the results and dangers of the system are disputed, but it is clear that it made for a very unusual modification to one of Morocco's Alpha Jets.

Luckily for us, Brandon Attard had the opportunity to photograph it! Look at the modified nose which holds the weather radar and the modification just visible under the wing on the aft fuselage. The Alpha Jet proved to be the best aircraft in the inventory for the operation, having no problem to fly at altitudes of over 8,000 meter over the clouds to drop the cartridges. Look at the light blue external fuel tanks on the outer wing pylons and the old style ejection Martin-Baker Mk.4 seats.

Photo: Philip Stevens

Photo: Peter Anthoni

Above: A French Alpha Jet flashes through the Wales' Mach loop at high speed. The pilot looks to be quite busy sitting in his Martin-Baker Mk.4 ejection seat.

Left: The pilot is putting his Armée de l'Air Alpha Jet through its paces and is performing a "dirty roll" - meaning that he is doing a roll with the landing gear out. Look at the position of the ailerons - can you make out what way the pilot is rolling the aircraft? The French Air Force continues to operate the Alpha Jet and currently has 57 in service, including those flying with the Patrouille de France. One thing you have to say about the aircraft: it doesn't show it's age !

Right: While the Alpha Jet is being refuelled - notice the fuel connection on the starboard side of the aircraft - this pilot is getting ready to step into the cockpit, all while looking extremely cool. Imagine getting paid to do that job!

Below: An Alpha Jet A with RAF roundels is banking hard to the left in the Mach Loop. The faded grey-green camouflage makes the aircraft look pretty cool. The jet is part of a flight of 6 that was active until 2018.

Photo: Robert Pied

Photo: Philip Stevens

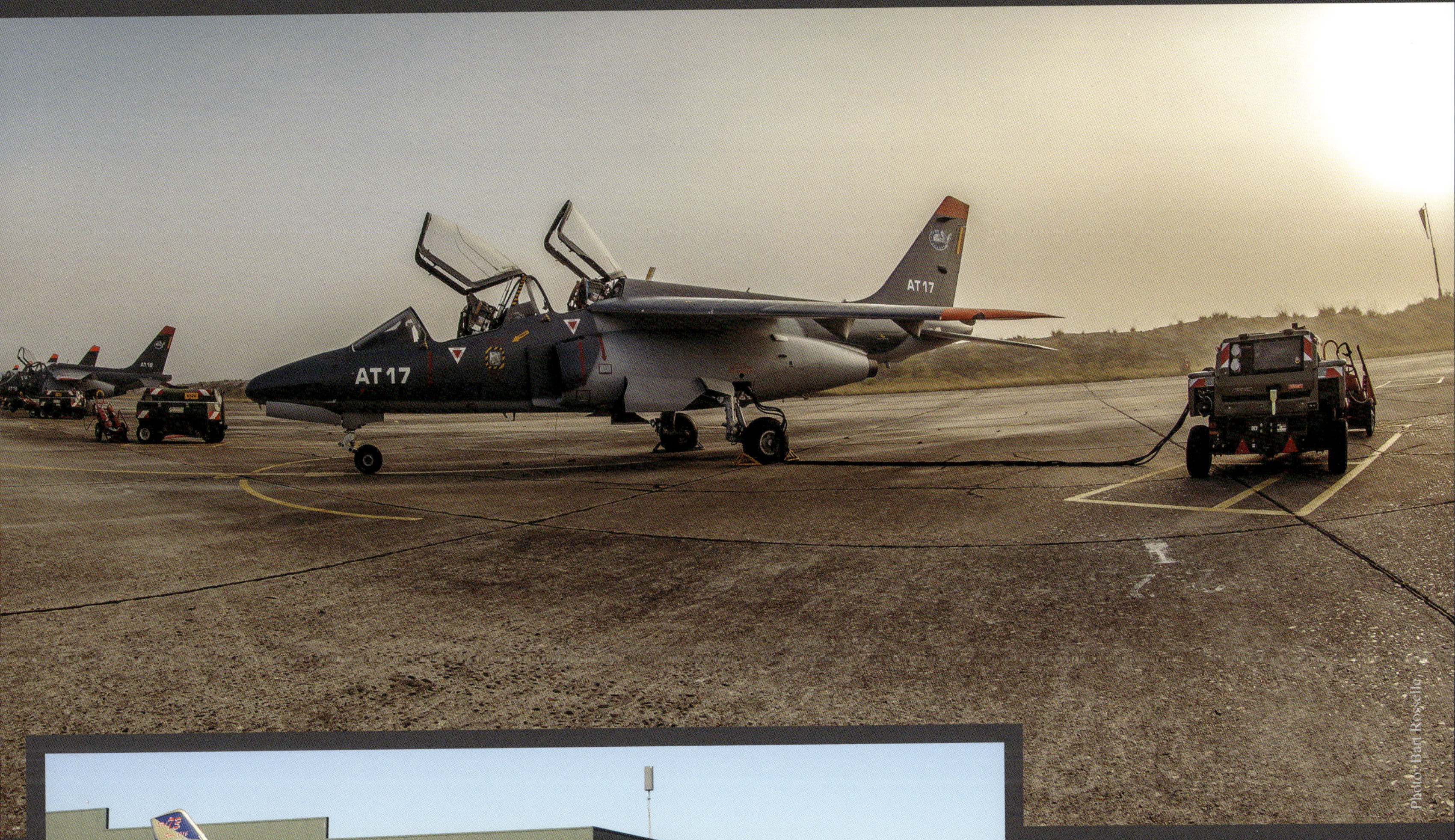

Photo: Bart Rosselle

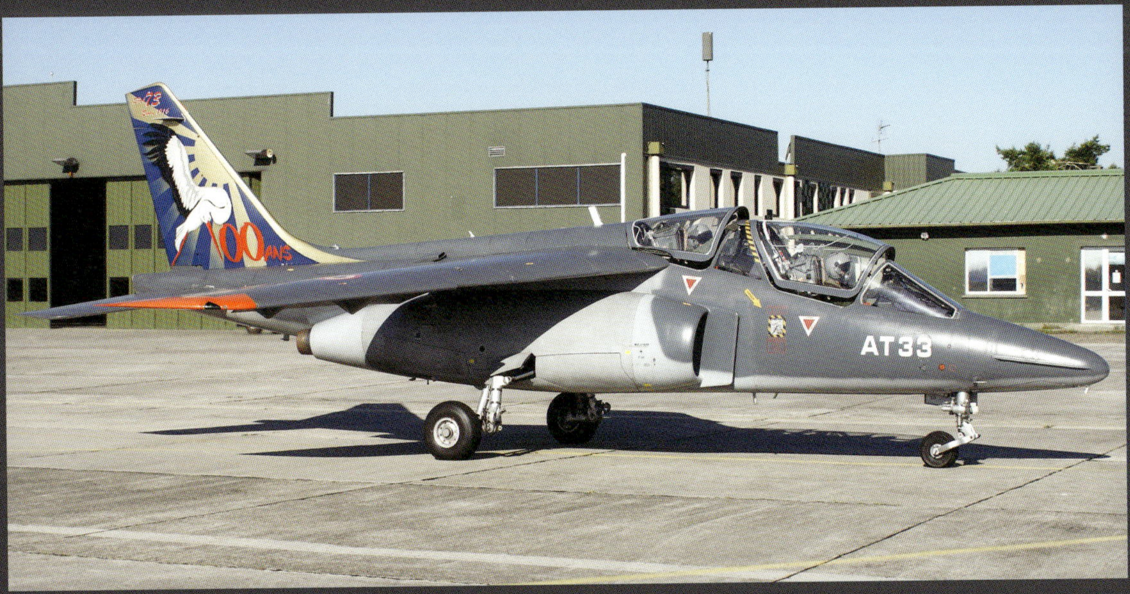

Photo: Robert Pied

Above: The morning sun pierces through the fog at Cazaux Air Base in France, where a line of Alpha Jets is waiting for another day of action. Another fantastic photo by Bart Rosselle !

Left: Here's a special one: A Belgian Air Force Alpha Jet sporting a special tail to celebrate the 100th anniversary of the French 73rd Squadron, a unit that was formed in the First World War, sporting the famous Stork emblem.

Photo: Peter Anthoni

Opposite page: The Patrouille de France trailing white smoke against a blue sky are coming out of a dive.
Below: While one Alpha Jet is moments away from touching down, 5 others are lined up on the tarmac, ready for a formation flight. Pilots are doing their pre-flight checks, while ground crew are making sure everything is the way it should be.

Above: Slow shutterspeed and a steady hand: this dynamic photo shows an Alpha Jet of the Patrouille de France landing at RAF Fairford for the annual Royal International Air Tattoo. Notice the new ejection seats and the light which is installed in the nose of the aircraft.
Right: Moments after returning from one of the final flights at Cazaux, Lt.Col. Marc Scheers looks out at the ramp. Look at the cool badge he's wearing on his shoulder.

Photo: Peter Anthoni

Photo: Robert Pied

Photo: Kris Christiaens

Photo: Jens Schymura

Above: No reason to put this photo in this book, other than that it is a fantastic one! There!

Right: A very smart Portuguese Alpha Jet A of 103 SQN is showing it's true colours when it's unzipped. In large letters EICPAC is written - Esquadra de Instrução Complementar de Pilotagem em Aviões de Combate. I'm sure you know what that translates into.

Left: What most student-pilots of the Belgian Air Force hope is the following step in their training, parked next to the Alpha Jet: An F-16B of the OCU - Operational Conversion Unit. If so, the skills that they have learned on the agile Alpha Jet will come in very useful. Notice the custom-made air intake and exhaust covers on this jet as well as the large number of remove-before-flight tags.

Photo: Peter Anthoni

Photo: Bart Rosselle

We end our book on the elegant jet trainer with another photo of this special one: the Belgian Air Force Alpha Jet AT-24 was the last one of the fleet to receive a special livery. By the end of 2018, the Belgian Air Force withdrew her fleet of Alpha Jets from active service. To commemorate the occasion, 40 years of service and 100 years of N° 11 Squadron, this livery was designed.

Called the "Dark Bat", the design was inspired by the "Dark Falcon", the F-16 of the Belgian Air Force F-16 Demo Team. One fun detail: the design of the Dark Bat was done by the the very same person that designs the Duke Hawkins books! Now tell me that isn't cool!

Duke

Duke
Hawkins

Doing a 116-page book on the Dassault/Dornier Alpha Jet might not be the most commercial thing to do, but when you take the time to have a closer look at the little jet, you'll notice that it is a beautiful and elegant aircraft, well worthy of an extensive photographic portrait. It was so much fun to make this book and to work with the many enthusiastic photographers that were involved. We want to thank all of them again - they are listed on page 4 - but also the people working at the air base of Beauvechain in Belgium for allowing us to visit them several times, sometimes on short notice. We also want to thank our contacts at the Cazaux air base, Lt. Col. Scheers and Bart Rosselle, who travelled to the base to make additional air-to-air shots of AT-24, the last Alpha Jet to receive a special decoration.

While you are reading this, we're already working on the next couple of books and we can tell you that we have some big surprises in store for you. As always, if you have suggestions, just send us an e-mail through our website. We hope you've enjoyed this 18th book in the series and thank you for buying it. By now, many of you have probably noticed that the back of the books form our logo, so why not collect them all?

Until the next book!

Duke